STECK-VAUGHN

BASIC
SCIENCE
FOR LIVING
EARTH AND LIFE SCIENCE

Jewel Varnado

**Steck-Vaughn
Company**
A Subsidiary of National Education Corporation

To the Teacher and the Student

Basic Science for Living is a two-book program specially designed for students who need to learn or review the basic scientific facts covered in a general science course. In *Earth and Life Science,* and *Physical Science,* students are introduced to science concepts through an explanation of the real-life science they experience every day. Students gain a thorough understanding of scientific terms and concepts from the relevant setting in which terms and concepts are presented. Mastering science is a challenging task. Special care has been taken in preparing both the organization and content of these books to guide the student to meeting this challenge with success.

- Each worktext is written in a manner that develops a high degree of reading comprehension and vocabulary, while providing a thorough survey of basic science. The author uses a conversational style of writing and consistent method of introducing, defining, and explaining scientific terms and processes to make the content lively, informative, and relevant for both student and teacher.

- Important science terms are highlighted and defined within the text. These terms are also defined and page referenced in a glossary at the back of each book.

- In each book, scientific facts and ideas have been grouped into seven units of related knowledge. *Earth and Life Science* begins with a discussion of the universe and our planet's place in the universe, then proceeds to discuss water, air, plants, animals, the human body, and health. *Physical Science* explores force and energy, thermal energy and heat, magnetism and electricity, light, sound, matter, and radioactivity and how these properties relate to our daily lives.

- Each unit is divided into several self-contained lessons. A review at the end of every lesson comprehensively tests the lesson's content. Lesson reviews follow five consistent, standardized formats that prepare students for other types of standardized assessment tools.

- Two black dots in the left margin of each lesson review signal critical thinking questions specially prepared to challenge students to apply knowledge they have gained to new situations.

- Each unit also presents two special features to make science more relevant to students lives. An *Issues in Science* lesson points out current science-related topics that are the subject of controversy or part of a trend in general science today. A *Careers* feature at the end of each unit points out careers in which general and/or specific science knowledge is important. Each career feature also provides a bibliography of books and associations for obtaining more information about careers in the area of science being discussed.

- A Mastery Review at the end of each book provides a chance to check mastery of important concepts and gives students practice with the commonly used separate-answer-sheet format. Clearly explained directions for the review allow it to be administered by the teacher or by students themselves.

- An easy-to-use Answer Key can be found at the back of each worktext. The answer key was prepared with both teacher and student use in mind. Students working independently will find the answer key an invaluable resource for checking their mastery of each lesson's concepts as presented in the lesson review. However, the answer key is perforated to allow easy removal for use in more traditional settings.

- The *Basic Science for Living* program was designed to bring science to students in a meaningful and useful way. The clarity of presentation, self-contained lessons, timely reviews, interesting features, glossary, mastery review, and answer key facilitate learning in a variety of educational situations—traditional classroom, small group seminar, tutorial instruction, and independent-study. The current and comprehensive content of *Basic Science for Living* provides students with the knowledge essential to understanding the world in which we live—a most exciting and interesting place.

About the Author

Jewel Varnado earned her bachelor's and master's degrees in educational psychology and her Ph.D. in adult education from Florida State University. She has received the Florida Adult Education Association's Outstanding Service Award and has successfully served as an instructor and a supervisor of adult education in Florida. She is the author of several children's books, a series of high-school English books *(English: Practice for Mastery),* and an English refresher course for adults *(English Essentials).*

ISBN 0-8114-4063-X

5 6 7 8 9 0 DBH 99 98 97 96 95 94 93

Contents

The Universe

Stars are one type of matter that makes up the universe.

Lesson 1

The Universe

The **universe** is made of all matter and energy and the space occupied by them. No one knows how large the universe is or, for that matter, if it has a definite size. Most scientists believe that the universe is constantly expanding. Others believe that the universe is expanding and contracting with time. Few scientists believe that the size of the universe is always the same.

How did the universe begin? There are many theories about its beginning. Theories are explanations that are backed by results that come from repeated tests or experiments. Today, most scientists who study the universe believe that it began with a **Big Bang.** According to this theory, an explosion about 15 billion years ago threw matter and energy in all directions. Much less than a second after the explosion, the universe was merely the size of a softball. As the original material cooled down from temperatures of billions

of degrees, it went through many other changes. These changes resulted in what we observe today as the universe—from the smallest atoms to the largest stars.

Several centuries ago, some astronomers, scientists who study space, believed that Earth was the center of the universe. It was thought that the moon, the sun and other stars, and the planets circled about Earth. Today, it is known that Earth is only a tiny speck in the universe. Planet Earth is part of a single galaxy. A **galaxy** is a large grouping of billions of stars, dust, and gas.

The galaxy that includes Earth is called the **Milky Way.** There are over a hundred billion stars in the Milky Way. The Milky Way is so large that it would take a beam of light traveling at 186,282 miles per second about 100,000 years to travel from one end of it to the other! The Milky Way is a disc-shaped galaxy with arms that turn about a dense center. Earth is located in one arm of the Milky Way, about 170,000,000,000,000,000 (170 quadrillion) miles from the center of the galaxy.

The part of our galaxy that includes Earth is called the solar system. The **solar system** includes the sun and all the natural objects that travel around it. In addition to Earth and eight other planets, the solar system contains asteroids, meteoroids, and comets.

Asteroids are fragments of matter similar to the matter that formed the planets. Asteroids are solid and have irregular shapes. They come in different sizes. The largest asteroid is nearly 500 miles in diameter. The smallest is less than a mile in diameter.

Meteoroids are small chunks of iron and rock. Most meteoroids probably form from collisions among asteroids. Some meteoroids enter Earth's atmosphere and burn up before they strike the ground. **Meteors** are streaks of light given off by these burning meteoroids. Meteoroids that reach Earth's surface without burning up are called **meteorites.**

Comets are masses of frozen gases, dust, and small pieces of rock. A comet has a solid head and a dust and gas tail. The tail of a comet points away from the sun. Halley's Comet is visible from Earth every 75 or 76 years.

The sun is the hub of our solar system. It is a huge star that is 330,000 times more massive than Earth. The sun is a very hot, bright sphere of gases. Our sun is an average star in terms of temperature and brightness when compared to other stars in the Milky Way. But to us, the sun is basic to life. We, along with other forms of life, are dependent upon its light and heat. Scientists estimate that the sun is about 4.5 billion years old. They believe that this nuclear furnace will exist for another 5 billion years. ■

Lesson Review

In the space before each number, write the letter of the word or group of words in Column 2 that matches the description in Column 1.

Column 1	Column 2
_____ 1. a large group of billions of stars, dust, and gases	a. asteroids
_____ 2. the light from meteoroids that burn up in Earth's atmosphere	b. Big Bang
_____ 3. fragments of matter ranging in size from less than a mile to 500 miles in diameter	c. comets
	d. galaxy
_____ 4. the sun and the other objects that travel around it	e. meteorites
_____ 5. masses of frozen gases, dust, and rocks	f. meteors
_____ 6. one theory on the origin of the universe	g. Milky Way
_____ 7. Earth's galaxy	h. solar system
_____ 8. meteoroids that strike Earth	i. sun
● _____ 9. all stars, planets, galaxies	j. universe
● _____ 10. star halfway through its life cycle	

The Planets

On a clear night, away from city lights, the sky above Earth glows with light. In addition to Earth's moon and countless stars, six of the eight other planets in our solar system are visible. Mercury, Venus, Mars, Jupiter, Saturn, and Uranus reflect light from the sun and thus are visible without the aid of a telescope. A star, like the sun, produces its own light. A planet is visible because light from the sun is reflected, or bounced, off its surface.

Like Earth, each planet moves in a set **orbit,** or circular path, around the sun. The orbits of the planets are oval-shaped. Therefore, a planet is closer to the sun at certain times and farther away at other times. Table 1 lists the average distance of each planet from the sun and Earth.

Mercury is the closest planet to the sun. However, it does not reflect much of the sunlight that falls on it and is difficult to see from Earth. Mercury's surface is made of flat, open areas and sharply rising cliffs. Numerous craters mark the landscape of the planet.

Venus is the second planet from the sun. Its diameter is about 400 miles less than Earth's. Venus receives about twice as much sunlight as Earth and is the brightest planet in the sky. Its average surface temperature is the highest of any planet in the solar system.

Earth is the third planet from the sun, followed by **Mars.** Viking spacecraft have been making observations of Mars since the mid-60s. The observations have shown that the Martian surface is made of steep ridges and valleys. Many volcanoes cover the rugged terrain. One of these, Olympus Mons, is the largest volcano in the solar system. The spacecraft observations have also shown that the polar caps of Mars are made of frozen carbon dioxide, or dry ice. A reddish dust gives Mars a pink hue.

Jupiter, the largest of the planets, is the fifth planet from the sun. The diameter of Jupiter is nearly 11 times that of Earth's. Scientists think that Jupiter is made of mostly hydrogen and helium gases, much like the

Table 1	**Facts About the Planets (All figures are approximate.)**				
	Average Distance in Miles from		**Time to Orbit Sun (in Earth-days and years)**	**Diameter in Miles**	**Average Surface Temperatures in Fahrenheit**	**Moons**
	Sun	**Earth**				
Mercury	36,000,000	57,000,000	88 days	3,031	550°F	0
Venus	66,800,000	25,700,000	225 days	7,520	900°F	0
Earth	93,000,000	----------	365 days	7,926	80°F	1
Mars	142,500,000	48,700,000	1.9 years	4,200	−76°F	2
Jupiter	480,000,000	390,700,000	12 years	88,700	−236°F	16
Saturn	888,000,000	762,700,000	29.5 years	74,980	−285°F	20
Uranus	1,700,000,000	1,700,000,000	84 years	31,570	−288°F	15
Neptune	2,754,000,000	2,821,000,000	165 years	30,200	−369°F	8
Pluto	3,666,000,000	3,583,000,000	248.5 years	~1,400	−387°F	1

sun. The planet is circled by white to reddish-brown cloud bands.

Saturn is the sixth planet from the sun. Although it is the second largest planet in our solar system, Saturn is not very dense. In fact, Saturn would float on water! More than 1,000 rings circle the planet and gleam with light.

Uranus and **Neptune** are the seventh and eighth planets from the sun. Voyager spacecraft have revealed that Uranus has at least ten rings around it and 15 satellites or moons. Neptune also is a gaseous planet. It is surrounded by dense clouds made of carbon dioxide and sulfur. Neptune has eight moons.

Pluto is often the most distant planet from the sun. Sometimes, however, Pluto orbits inside the orbit of Neptune. Pluto is thought to be made of frozen water and gases. Pluto has a single moon.

Many people wonder if there is life on the other planets in our solar system. The average surface temperatures listed in Table 1 clearly show that life as we know it here on Earth could not exist on the other planets. Other forms of life, however, may exist. Perhaps some day we will know. ■

Lesson Review

Fill in the circle containing the letter of the term or phrase that correctly completes each statement. Check Table 1 to answer some of the questions.

1. All of the following planets are visible from Earth except _____.
   ⓐ Mercury   ⓑ Mars   ⓒ Venus   ⓓ Pluto

2. _____ are visible because they reflect light from their surfaces.
   ⓐ Stars   ⓑ Planets   ⓒ Orbits   ⓓ Viking spacecraft

3. The closest planet to the sun is _____.
   ⓐ Pluto   ⓑ Earth   ⓒ Venus   ⓓ Mercury

4. The average surface temperature of _____ is the highest of any planet.
   ⓐ Earth   ⓑ Mercury   ⓒ Pluto   ⓓ Venus

5. The polar caps of Mars are made of _____.
   ⓐ frozen water   ⓑ frozen carbon dioxide   ⓒ helium   ⓓ hydrogen

6. _____ is the largest planet in our solar system.
   ⓐ Pluto   ⓑ Saturn   ⓒ Neptune   ⓓ Jupiter

7. Although it is the second largest planet, _____ would float on water.
   ⓐ Saturn   ⓑ Earth   ⓒ Venus   ⓓ Mars

8. _____ is usually the outermost planet in our solar system.
   ⓐ Mercury   ⓑ Neptune   ⓒ Pluto   ⓓ Venus

● 9. _____ and _____ have hotter temperatures than Earth.
   ⓐ Saturn, Mars   ⓑ Mercury, Venus   ⓒ Uranus, Neptune   ⓓ Mars, Venus

● 10. The planets _____ and _____ will never complete their orbits in a human's lifetime.
   ⓐ Earth, Venus   ⓑ Jupiter, Uranus   ⓒ Neptune, Pluto   ⓓ Pluto, Mercury

Earth's Moon

The moon is Earth's only natural satellite. A **satellite** is an object that revolves around a larger, primary object. Much of what we know about our moon comes from observations made by spacecraft. An uncrewed Soviet spacecraft landed on the moon in 1959. Ten years later, an American spacecraft, Apollo 11, with astronauts aboard landed on the lunar surface. This and five other Apollo landings allowed astronauts to gather samples of the lunar soil and rocks. Today, scientists continue to examine these samples.

The moon appears larger than most of the planets in the solar system because it is so close to Earth. At the shortest point in its orbit, the moon is about 220,000 miles from Earth. At its farthest distance, the moon is over 250,000 miles away. (Venus, the planet closest to Earth, is over 25 million miles away.)

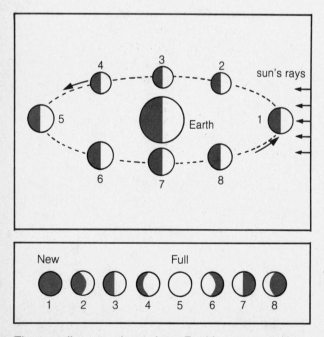

New   Full
1 2 3 4 5 6 7 8

The top diagram shows how Earth's moon would look to an observer in space. The bottom diagram illustrates the moon as it appears to an observer on Earth.

Although the moon appears large, it is really quite small. It has a diameter of 2,160 miles, about one-quarter of Earth's diameter.

Gravity is the attraction between two objects due to their masses. The pull of gravity among Earth, the moon, and the sun causes tides. The moon's gravity causes a bulge of ocean water on the side of Earth that faces the moon. A second bulge forms on the side of Earth away from the moon. The bulges of water are called high tides. The area between the bulges is called low tide. The tides at a particular place rise and fall as Earth turns. Most coastal areas on Earth have two high tides and two low tides each day.

It takes the moon about $27\frac{1}{3}$ days to **revolve** around, or circle, Earth. The moon's **rotation**, or spinning about its axis, also takes about $27\frac{1}{3}$ days. Therefore, because both its rotation and revolution take the same amount of time, an observer on Earth always sees the same side of the moon. Due to the tilt of the moon's axis at different times, an observer can see about 59 percent of its surface by watching the moon over a period of time. No one had ever seen the dark side of the moon until pictures were sent back to Earth in 1959.

Many of the features of the side of the moon that could be seen were known before spacecraft landed. Early astronomers discovered that the moon's surface was made up of dark areas and light areas. The dark areas are smooth, flat plains; the light areas are rocky and mountainous.

Craters, bowl-shaped areas on the moon's surface, have been clearly visible through telescopes since the 1600s. Craters range in size from less than one mile to over 150 miles in diameter. Most of the moon's craters formed when meteoroids struck the moon's surface billions of years ago. Because the moon has no atmosphere, there is no weather to change its surface. Most of the craters have not changed since they were formed.

Before astronauts explored the moon, people imagined what it would be like to visit. From the moon, astronomers would have a better view of the universe. Scientists could study the moon firsthand. The average vacationer, however, probably would not want to rush to the moon. The moon has no atmosphere and no water. Human beings can't breathe on its surface. Average temperatures during the two-week lunar day reach 270°F and plunge during the 14-day lunar night to −250°F. Due to the moon's weak gravity, a person who weighs about 100 pounds on Earth would weigh less than 20 pounds on the moon. Living on the moon would be very inconvenient! ■

Lesson Review

Fill in the circle containing the letter of the term or phrase that correctly completes each statement.

1. A(n) _____ is an object that revolves around a larger, primary object.
   - (a) orbit
   - (b) satellite
   - (c) spacecraft
   - (d) axis

2. The moon appears larger than most of the planets in our solar system because _____.
   - (a) it is larger than all the planets except Pluto
   - (b) its rotation equals its revolution
   - (c) it is a satellite of Earth
   - (d) it is close to Earth

3. _____ is the attraction between two objects due to their masses.
   - (a) Orbit
   - (b) Gravity
   - (c) Tide
   - (d) Rotation

4. Tides occur on Earth due to the gravity among _____.
   - (a) the sun, moon, and Earth
   - (b) the sun and moon
   - (c) the sun and Earth
   - (d) the sun, Earth, and other planets

5. To an observer on Earth, almost _____ percent of the moon's surface is visible.
   - (a) 10
   - (b) 25
   - (c) 60
   - (d) 75

6. The dark areas of the moon are _____.
   - (a) mountains
   - (b) bodies of water
   - (c) plains
   - (d) shadows cast by Earth

7. Lunar craters formed billions of years ago when _____ struck the moon's surface.
   - (a) spacecraft
   - (b) volcanoes
   - (c) water
   - (d) meteroids

8. A lunar day is about _____ long.
   - (a) 12 hours
   - (b) 24 hours
   - (c) 14 days
   - (d) 27 days

● 9. The diameter of Earth is about _____ times _____ than the diameter of the moon.
   - (a) 3, larger
   - (b) 4, larger
   - (c) 3, smaller
   - (d) 4, smaller

● 10. To an observer on Earth, the moon orbits Earth from _____.
   - (a) east to west
   - (b) west to east
   - (c) south to north
   - (d) north to south

Earth's Profile

Earth is about 4.5 billion years old. There are several theories about its formation. Most scientists believe that the sun, Earth, and the other planets formed from a slowly spinning, gigantic cloud of dust and gas.

Thanks to various branches of science, we have learned a great deal about Earth. The highest point on Earth is Mt. Everest. It towers over 29,000 feet above **sea level**. Sea level is defined as zero feet elevation. The lowest point on Earth is in the Pacific Ocean. It is in an underwater canyon called the Mariana Trench. The canyon's lowest point is more than 36,000 feet below sea level. Scientists, using mathematics rather than a scale, have calculated that Earth weighs over six sextillion (6,000,000,000,000,000,000,000) tons!

From space, Earth appears to be a perfect sphere. In reality, however, it is slightly flattened at its poles. The diameter of Earth from the North Pole to the South Pole is about 7,900 miles. The **equator** is an imaginary line that separates Earth into two hemispheres: the Northern Hemisphere and the Southern Hemisphere. Earth's diameter at the equator is roughly 7,926 miles.

Look closely at a globe of Earth. Earth has been called the "Blue Planet" because almost three fourths of Earth is covered with water. Although water is the most common substance found on Earth, only three percent of Earth's water is drinkable. Most of Earth's water is salt water contained in the oceans.

Earth's surface area totals almost 197 million square miles. Of this total, less than 58 million square miles is land. Plains, plateaus, and mountains are the three basic landforms that cover Earth's surface. **Plains** are large, flat, low-lying areas. The Great Plains extend through much of the central United States. **Plateaus** are high, relatively flat areas. The Colorado Plateau, into which the Grand Canyon was carved, is located in the western United States. **Mountains** are any area of land that rises sharply above the surrounding area. The Appalachians, the Rockies, and the Great Smoky Mountains are only a few of the mountain chains in the United States.

Although we can't feel it, planet Earth is constantly in motion. Earth moves in three ways. It rotates, or spins on its axis, once every 24 hours. Day and night are caused by Earth's rotation. As it rotates, Earth also revolves around the sun. Earth's revolution takes about $365\frac{1}{4}$ days, or one year, to complete. Earth also moves in a third way through space. Together with the sun and the other planets in our solar system, it travels around the center of its galaxy, the Milky Way. Earth completes this journey once every 225 million years.

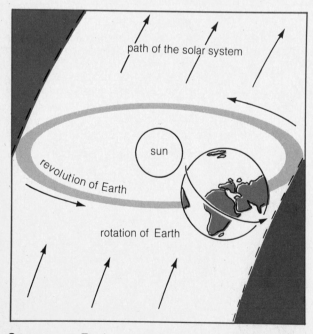

path of the solar system

sun

revolution of Earth

rotation of Earth

Seasons on Earth are due to the tilt of Earth's axis and the angle at which the sun's rays strike a given location.

Recall that Earth's orbit, or revolution, around the sun is oval-shaped. In January, Earth is about 88,000,000 miles from the sun. In July, Earth is about 91,000,000 miles from the sun. Why then is it hotter in the United States in July than in January?

The seasons occur for two reasons. First, Earth's axis is tilted about $23\frac{1}{2}$ degrees. This tilt causes the amount of daylight to vary at a given location. Secondly, the angle at which the sun's rays strike a certain location changes throughout the year. Refer to the illustration. When the North Pole is tilted toward the sun, the Northern Hemisphere has summer. At this time, the Southern Hemisphere has winter. When the North Pole is tilted away from the sun, the Northern Hemisphere has winter. Therefore, at the end of December, it is winter in Minneapolis, Minnesota, and summer in Santiago, Chile.

Earth is a dynamic planet. It changes constantly in response to the many forces and processes acting upon it. Hurricanes, tornadoes, thunderstorms, landslides, ocean waves, volcanic eruptions, earthquakes, rivers, lakes, and streams are just a few of the agents that change our planet daily. Some of these changes are quite noticeable; others take millions of years to occur. ■

Lesson Review

In the space provided, write the word or words that best complete the statement.

1. Earth is about _____ years old.

2. The highest point on Earth is _____.

3. Earth's shape is _____.

4. Nearly _____ of Earth's surface is covered with water.

5. _____ are large, flat, low-lying areas.

6. Earth _____ on its axis once every 24 hours.

7. Earth is closest to the sun in the month of _____.

8. Seasons occur due to the tilt of Earth's axis and the change in _____

_____.

● 9. If it is winter at the South Pole, it is _____ at the North Pole.

● 10. The amount of relief, or change in elevation, between Mt. Everest and the Mariana Trench is _____ feet.

The Structure of Earth

Geology is the study of planet Earth and the processes that change it. Geologists are scientists who study the origin, history, and structure of our planet. Geologists have learned that shortly after it formed, parts of the inside of Earth melted. Denser materials sank to Earth's center. Lighter materials floated upward. With time, these materials hardened to form our planet.

Geologists divide Earth into three distinct layers. The innermost region of Earth is called the **core.** A molten, or partly melted, outer core surrounds a solid inner core. The inner core is rich in iron and nickel and has a diameter of about 1,500 miles. Temperatures here may be as high as 9,000°F. Earth's outer core has a diameter of about 2,800 miles. Temperatures in the outer core are about 4,000°F.

Surrounding the core is the **mantle,** or middle layer, of Earth. Much of the mantle is solid. At depths of about 60 to 400 miles, the mantle is partly melted and acts like putty. The mantle is about 1,800 miles thick and makes up over 80 percent of Earth's volume.

The outer layer of Earth is called the **crust.** Its thickness varies between three and 22 miles. The crust that makes up the continents averages over 20 miles in thickness. Ocean crust is about three miles thick.

Rocks make up much of Earth's crust, mantle, and core. Geologists classify rocks into three groups: igneous, sedimentary, and metamorphic. **Igneous rocks** form when hot, molten material cools and hardens. If the material cools below Earth's suface, rocks such as granite are formed. If the molten material reaches Earth's surface through erupting volcanoes, then lava and pumice may form.

Sedimentary rocks are rocks that form when pieces of material, such as clay and sand,

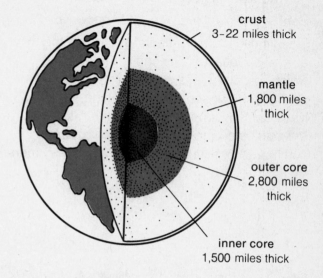

crust
3–22 miles thick

mantle
1,800 miles thick

outer core
2,800 miles thick

inner core
1,500 miles thick

Earth can be divided into three layers: the crust, the mantle, and the core.

become cemented together by natural processes. Sedimentary rocks can form in water or on land. **Fossils,** the remains of animals and plants preserved in Earth's crust, are commonly found in sedimentary rocks.

Metamorphic rocks are rocks that are changed by intense heat and pressure. Marble is the metamorphic equivalent of the sedimentary rock, limestone. Slate is metamorphosed shale. Gneiss is metamorphosed granite.

The continents are parts of the rocky crust that covers about one fourth of Earth's surface. Look closely at a world map. Compare the eastern coastline of South America with the west coast of Africa. Notice the puzzlelike fit of the edges of these continents. Scientists have attempted to explain why, when moved around and rotated, the continents seem to fit together like pieces of a puzzle. This evidence, and fossil, climate, and rock-structure data, led scientists to conclude that the continents were once a single landmass. But how could such massive pieces of land move such great distances?

The theory of **plate tectonics** states that Earth's crust and upper mantle are divided into large sections called plates. Scientists recognize ten major plates and about a dozen smaller ones. These plates are driven by powerful forces within Earth over the puttylike portion of the mantle. According to the theory, the continents are "passengers" on the moving plates, much like items on a conveyor belt.

Plates move very slowly, from between half an inch to over seven inches per year. Plates can collide, move apart, or move horizontally past one another. Mountains, volcanoes, and earthquakes are just a few results of plate movements. In most cases, when two plates collide, mountains are formed.

Plates move horizontally past one another along large fractures in Earth's surface called **faults.** Earthquakes are very common along faults because of the enormous pressure that builds up between the moving plates. ■

Lesson Review

On the line before each statement, write the letter of the choice that best completes the statement.

_____ 1. After Earth formed, parts of the inside of Earth _____.

    a. froze   b. melted   c. disappeared   d. collided

_____ 2. Earth's inner core is _____.

    a. solid   c. surrounded by a molten outer core

    b. rich in nickel and iron   d. all of the above

_____ 3. The _____ makes up most of Earth's volume.

    a. crust   b. mantle   c. outer core   d. inner core

_____ 4. _____ rocks form from molten material.

    a. Igneous   b. Sedimentary   c. Metamorphic   d. All of the above

_____ 5. Limestone is a(n) _____ rock.

    a. igneous   b. sedimentary   c. metamorphic   d. volcanic

_____ 6. _____ data led scientists to conclude that the present day continents were once a single landmass.

    a. Fossil   b. Climate   c. Rock structure   d. All of the above

_____ 7. Plates are large sections of Earth's _____.

    a. inner and outer core   c. crust and upper mantle

    b. upper and lower mantle   d. mantle and core

_____ 8. Plates move on the puttylike portion of the _____.

    a. crust   b. mantle   c. outer core   d. inner core

• _____ 9. The _____ is the densest layer of Earth.

    a. crust   b. upper mantle   c. lower mantle   d. core

• _____ 10. The Alps, a mountain range in Europe, formed when two plates _____.

    a. moved apart   b. sank   c. collided   d. faulted

Mapping Planet Earth

As early as about 500 B.C., a Greek philosopher, Pythagoras, concluded that Earth was a sphere. In 150 A.D., a scholar named Ptolemy used this information to divide a circle representing Earth into 360 equal parts. Each part was called a degree. Each degree can be divided into minutes. Sixty minutes equals one degree.

Look at a globe or map of Earth. Note that an imaginary grid of intersecting lines covers the globe or map. These lines can be used to pinpoint any place on Earth's surface. Lines running east-west are called **parallels** or **lines of latitude.** The lines that run north-south are called **meridians** or **lines of longitude.**

Recall that the equator is an imaginary line that divides Earth into two equal hemispheres. The equator is 0° (zero degrees) latitude. Locations north or south of the equator are numbered 10°, 20°, 30°, and so on. Each pole is at 90°. Parallels north of the equator are designated as north latitudes. Those south of the equator are south latitudes.

Just as the equator is used as a reference point for lines of latitude, the **prime meridian** is designated 0° longitude. By international agreement, the prime meridian runs through a point where the British Royal Observatory was once located in a section of London called Greenwich. Points west of the prime meridian have west longitude. Points east of the prime meridian have east longitude. The west and east lines of longitude meet at the 180° meridian or the International Date Line. The International Date Line is directly opposite the prime meridian and runs through the Pacific Ocean. The International Date Line is used by most countries of the world to keep time. The International Date Line is 12 time zones from the prime meridian. Thus, when it is one minute after 12:00 noon on Friday in Greenwich, it is one minute after 12:00 midnight on Saturday at the 180° meridian.

Refer to the map on page 15. Note that the lines of latitude and longitude are spaced at intervals of 5°. Also note that each line of latitude and longitude is divided into minutes. For example, the line of latitude marked 45°00′ is read as "45 degrees, zero minutes." A location halfway between the 45°00′ and 50°00′ lines of latitude would be designated 47°30′. Find New York City on the map. New York City is located at approximately 41°N latitude and 74°W longitude. What do the letters "N" and "W" mean? New York City is located north (N) of the equator and west (W) of the prime meridian. What is the approximate location of Houston, Texas?

Recall that Earth is a sphere flattened at the poles. Thus the distances between lines of latitude and longitude are not exactly the same at every point on a globe. The distance between two degrees of latitude near the poles is a little less than 69 miles. Near the equator, this distance is a little more than 69 miles. The distance between two degrees of longitude near Mobile, Alabama, is about 70 miles. Farther north, near Grand Forks, North Dakota, the distance is about 68 miles.

The science of mapmaking is **cartography.** People who make maps are called cartographers. Today, even with photographs taken from artificial satellites miles above Earth's surface and with the aid of computers, cartographers have a difficult job making maps. One reason is because Earth's surface is always changing. Therefore, maps quickly become dated. Also, it is difficult to represent a three-dimensional, spherical object like Earth on a flat piece of paper. ■

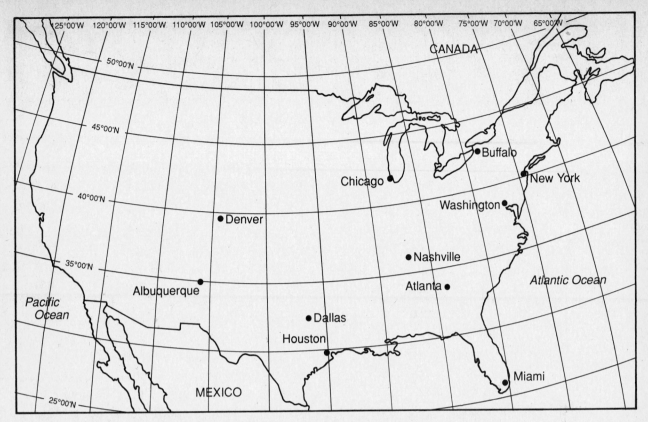

Lines of latitude and longitude are used to pinpoint any location on Earth's surface.

Lesson Review

In the space before each number, write the letter of the word or group of words in Column 2 that matches the description in Column 1. Use the map above when necessary.

Column 1	Column 2
_____ 1. science of mapmaking	a. cartography
_____ 2. sixty minutes	b. Chicago
_____ 3. lines of latitude	c. degree
_____ 4. zero degrees latitude	d. Denver
_____ 5. zero degrees longitude	e. equator
_____ 6. American city at about 80°W longitude	f. International Date Line
_____ 7. American city at about 40°N latitude	g. Miami
_____ 8. meridian used for world time	h. parallels
• _____ 9. 90°S latitude	i. prime meridian
• _____ 10. American city at about 42°N latitude, 87°W longitude	j. South Pole

15

Twenty years ago, a conservation group made a surprising discovery. They found out that on Memorial Day, picnickers all over the United States threw away an amazing amount of litter. People tossed out enough litter to make a wall two feet wide, four inches high, and 3,000 miles long. Today, that 3,000 mile-long wall would be 12 feet wide and two feet high! The disposal of solid wastes has become a world problem.

Solid wastes include paper, plastic, glass and other containers, garbage, foam containers and packing materials, and junked automobiles. Each person in the United States throws away over six pounds of solid wastes each day. Where will we put all these wastes? How will these wastes affect the environment? Who will pay for their disposal? It is estimated that the cost of disposing of solid wastes in the United States is approaching $20 billion a year.

For many years, open dumps were the most common way of getting rid of solid wastes. Solid wastes were hauled to a dump and left there. Open dumps not only ruin the appearance of an area, but they also serve as breeding grounds for rats and other disease-spreading animals. Organic wastes left in open dumps rot and smell horribly. Water draining through open dumps can introduce harmful chemicals into streams and ground water.

Sanitary landfills offer a way to dispose of solid waste that does little damage to the places where they are located. In a properly run landfill, tractors pack down each day's solid wastes and cover the wastes with soil. This method stops insects and other animals from getting into the wastes. It also speeds up the decomposition, or breaking down, of solid wastes. Many sanitary landfills, however, are not run properly. Also, sooner or later they outgrow the areas set aside for them. Many landfills have had to be closed because they have reached their capacities. To protect the environment, many communities and states have passed strict laws for their use.

How do solid wastes affect planet Earth? A large percentage of solid wastes do not decompose, or break down. At one time, steel containers were used for many products. When thrown out, these containers eventually rusted and became part of the soil. Today, however, aluminum containers have replaced most of the steel containers. Aluminum takes years and years to degrade, or decompose. Plastics present a similar problem.

Incineration, or burning, is another common method for getting rid of solid wastes. However, it must be done in such a way that harmful substances do not enter and pollute Earth's atmosphere. A properly operated incinerator is too expensive for most communities. As a result, in many areas, regional incinerators have been built either by the government or by private companies. Each community then establishes a **transfer station,** a place where solid wastes are brought and stored for a short period of time. Compactors pack the trash tightly. Then it is picked up and trucked to the regional incinerator. This method does very little harm to the environment, but it is expensive. Hauling costs can easily approach $65 a ton.

Earth's space for storing and getting rid of solid wastes is limited. This has led many people to **recycle,** or reuse, many things. Some solid wastes, such as paper, glass, metal, and wood fiber, can be recycled. In many parts of the country, people separate these items from the rest of their trash. Newspapers, clear glass, colored glass, and aluminum are placed in separate bins located in certain areas of a transfer station. These recyclable items are then picked up and paid for by companies that recycle them. Recycling reduces the cost of hauling and burning solid wastes. Through recycling, a community's solid waste gains income for the community.

Unfortunately, many solid wastes, including most plastics, are not recyclable. Scientists are currently doing research to develop biodegradable plastics. These plastics are decomposed by bacteria into compounds that do not harm the environment.

Earth is a fragile planet. The number of people living on Earth will probably exceed 8 billion by 2050. How will people cope with the increased demand on our planet's resources? How will the disposal of solid wastes from so many people be achieved? These are questions that everyone has to face. ■

Lesson Review

Fill in the circle containing the letter of the term or phrase that correctly completes each statement.

1. The problem with most solid wastes is that they _____.
   - (a) take up a lot of space
   - (b) contaminate the soil
   - (c) are nondegradable
   - (d) all of the above

2. Each person in the United States throws away over _____ pounds of solid wastes each day.
   - (a) two
   - (b) four
   - (c) five
   - (d) six

3. Water draining through _____ can introduce harmful chemicals into streams and other water sources.
   - (a) open dumps
   - (b) soils
   - (c) discarded wood
   - (d) incinerators

4. Each of the following is an example of solid waste except _____.
   - (a) paper
   - (b) junk automobiles
   - (c) glass bottles
   - (d) sewage

5. Solid wastes in a sanitary landfill must be covered with _____.
   - (a) water
   - (b) soil
   - (c) more trash
   - (d) nondegradable waste

6. Incineration of solid wastes must be done correctly so that harmful substances do not enter _____.
   - (a) the atmosphere
   - (b) the soil
   - (c) rivers and streams
   - (d) incinerators

7. A(n) _____ is a place where solid wastes are brought and held temporarily.
   - (a) sanitary landfill
   - (b) open dump
   - (c) transfer station
   - (d) incinerator

8. _____ can dramatically lower the cost of solid waste disposal.
   - (a) Hauling
   - (b) Incineration
   - (c) Soil covering
   - (d) Recycling

● 9. _____ can aid the recycling effort.
   - (a) Weather
   - (b) Plastic wrappers
   - (c) Deposits on bottles
   - (d) Larger landfills

● 10. Each of the following is degradable except _____.
   - (a) steel cans
   - (b) newspapers
   - (c) foam containers
   - (d) wooden crates

Surveyors work closely with civil engineers to establish exact boundaries for roads, highways, and bridges.

Astronomers are scientists who study the universe. Using their knowledge of mathematics, physics, and geology, they seek a better understanding of the stars, planets, and other objects that make up the universe. Some astronomers observe the objects in the universe through telescopes, but most rely on photographs and electronic detecting equipment for their observations. Most astronomers teach at colleges and universities. Some work in research organizations and observatories. NASA, the National Aeronautics and Space Administration, a federal agency that oversees the United States space program, also employs astronomers.

Geologists study the history of planet Earth and the various processes that change it. Some geologists work for industries that are engaged in mining coal and mineral deposits. Some geologists search for oil and gas. These scientists use their knowledge of how Earth was formed and changed in the past 4.5 billion years to locate areas where precious rocks and minerals and oil and natural gas are likely to be found. Many geologists are employed by the federal government and work for such agencies as the United States Geological Survey, the Forest Service, the National Park Service, and the Soil Conservation Service.

Cartographers use papers, pencils, drafting tools, and computers to produce the many general reference maps and special maps that people rely on for a variety of information. They work with surveyors, geologists, drafters, and various other experts to produce accurate maps and charts. Many cartographers work for such government agencies as the Defense Department, the United States Geological Survey, and the National Oceanic and Atmospheric Administration, or NOAA. Some work for commercial mapmakers and for nonprofit organizations, such as the National Geographic Society.

Surveyors identify and measure land and water boundaries, gather information for deeds and other legal documents, and measure construction sites. They work closely with civil engineers to establish the exact boundaries for roads, highways, and bridges. Surveyors are always a part of the mapmaking process. Most work for private engineering firms, and some work for local and state governments.

In all areas of earth science, many opportunities exist for those who have some technical background. Astronomical observatories employ a variety of workers who maintain equipment and assist professional staff members. Geologists often use field assistants for a variety of tasks. Drafters, artists, and researchers are essential to the mapmaking industry. ∎

For Further Information

More information about these and related careers is available from the following publications and organizations.

Career Opportunities in Geology and the Earth Sciences, Linda A. Rossbacher, Arco, 1983

Maps and Mapmakers, R. Tooley, Crown, 1978

Drafting As a Career, American Institute for Design and Drafting, 1982

A Career in Astronomy, American Astronomical Society, 1982

American Astronomical Society
University of Delaware
Newark, DE 19711

American Geophysical Union
2000 Florida Avenue, NW
Washington, DC 20009

Water

On Earth, water can exist as a gas, a liquid, or a solid. What state of matter is shown in the photograph above?

Water Is Matter

Most animals and many plants can live out of water, but they cannot live without water. Water is needed by all living things. This basic substance is composed of two parts hydrogen (H), and one part oxygen (O). The chemical formula of water is H_2O.

Water is a unique substance. On Earth, water is the only matter that occurs naturally in three states. **Matter** is anything that has mass and takes up space. On our planet, water occurs as a liquid, a solid, and a gas.

A **liquid** is the state of matter that has a constant volume, but no fixed shape. Water at room temperature is a liquid. A quart of water always fills a quart-sized container, no matter what the shape of the container. A **solid** is the state of matter that has both a definite shape and a definite volume. Frozen water, or ice, is a solid. A **gas** is the state of matter that has no fixed volume or shape.

Steam, or water vapor, is a gas. A certain volume of steam can be condensed and placed into a pint-sized container, or it can expand to fill a gallon-sized container.

Why is a liquid a liquid? a solid a solid? a gas a gas? All matter is made of very tiny particles that are constantly in motion. The state of matter depends on two factors: the amount of space between the particles and the motion of the particles. In a solid, the particles are very close together. Forces among the particles in a solid allow them to vibrate but do not allow the particles to change positions. In a liquid, the particles also are very close together. The forces that hold the particles together, however, aren't as strong as those in solids. Therefore, the particles in a liquid are able to change positions. In a gas, particles are very far apart from one another. Forces cannot hold the particles in place. Therefore, the particles that make up a gas move freely.

How does matter change its state? Changes in temperature can cause most forms of matter to change state. **Evaporation** is the process by which a liquid changes to a gas. The temperature at which a liquid becomes a gas is called the boiling point. The boiling point of water at sea level is 212°F.

Condensation is the process by which a gas changes to a liquid. Fog is the result of the condensation of water vapor in Earth's atmosphere. **Melting** is the process by which a solid changes to a liquid. It occurs at a temperature called the melting point. The melting point of ice is 32°F.

Solidification is the process by which a liquid changes to a solid. The temperature at which this change takes place is the freezing point. The freezing point of water is 32°F. During solidification, many materials contract. However, when pure water is cooled, it contracts until it reaches 39°F. As it cools further, the water expands rapidly as it nears its freezing point. This expansion in the final phase of solidification causes many water-filled containers, such as glass, to burst as the water changes to ice. Expansion of water during solidification also makes ice less dense than water. Therefore, ice floats in water.

Some solids can change into gases without becoming liquids. The change from a solid to a gas or a gas to a solid with no liquid phase is sublimation. Frost occurs when water vapor sublimes, or changes, to ice.

Nearly three fourths of Earth is covered by water. Oceans, seas, lakes, rivers, streams, ponds, and other bodies of water are liquid states of water. **Glaciers** are vast masses of ice in motion. Water vapor is present in Earth's atmosphere in amounts that vary between zero and four percent by volume. Condensation, evaporation, and solidification of water allow it to circulate over our planet. This exchange of water among Earth's land, water bodies, and atmosphere is the **water cycle.** ■

Lesson Review

Determine whether each of the following statements is true or false. Correct each false statement by crossing out the word or phrase that makes it false and writing the correct word or phrase above it.

_____ 1. The chemical formula of water is H_2O.

_____ 2. Matter is anything that has weight and takes up space.

_____ 3. A liquid has no fixed shape and a fixed volume.

_____ 4. A gas is the state of matter that has both a definite shape and a definite volume.

_____ 5. All matter is made of tiny particles that are in motion.

_____ 6. A liquid evaporates at its boiling point.

_____ 7. The freezing point of water is 100°F.

_____ 8. Frost is the result of the sublimation of a gas to a solid.

● _____ 9. Icebergs float due to the contraction of water as the water freezes.

● _____ 10. Seeing your breath in the winter is an example of melting.

The Water Planet

Recall that water is always in motion on planet Earth. Water, no matter what its state, moves among Earth's land, bodies of water, and atmosphere. This never-ending circulation of water is the water cycle. The water cycle is powered by energy from the sun.

How does water move through the water cycle? The heat of the sun evaporates water from oceans, rivers, streams, lakes, ponds, and puddles, and produces water vapor. As the water vapor rises, it cools and condenses to form tiny drops of liquid water. **Clouds** are collections of millions of water droplets suspended in the atmosphere. Water droplets in clouds may join until they get so heavy that they can no longer stay suspended. Then, depending on certain atmospheric conditions, they fall to Earth as rain, snow, sleet, or hail. Rain, snow, sleet, and hail are forms of **precipitation.**

Most precipitation falls over the oceans. Some of this moisture falls into rivers and lakes. The rest of it falls over land. Much of the moisture that reaches Earth's surface runs off the land. Some of it soaks into the ground and becomes ground water. Most precipitation slowly makes its way back to the ocean and the water cycle begins again.

Plants play an important role in the water cycle. Trees and other plants take water from the soil through their roots and expel it from their leaves in a process called transpiration. Some trees lose about four gallons of water to the atmosphere per hour on a hot, sunny day.

Oceans cover about 70 percent of Earth and account for about 95 percent of all its water! Like the atmosphere, an ocean is a mixture of solids, liquids, and gases. Most of the materials in ocean water are ions. **Ions** are atoms with electrical charges. The chloride ion

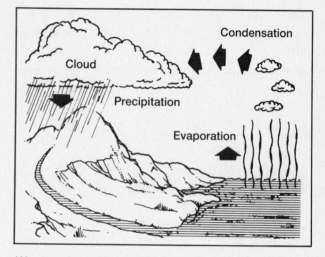

Water moves along Earth's land, water bodies, and atmosphere in the water cycle.

(Cl^-) and the sodium ion (Na^+) make up about 85 percent of the dissolved materials in ocean water. When these two ions combine, they form sodium chloride, common table salt. One cubic mile of ocean water contains about 166 million tons of salt! Because the ocean is so "salty," it is more dense than fresh water.

Ocean water also contains magnesium, carbon, calcium, iodine, iron, zinc, and over 50 other elements. The source of many of these elements is Earth's crust. As rivers make their way to the oceans, they erode, or wear away, some components of the crust and deposit these materials in the oceans.

Only about three percent of Earth's water is fresh water. Two-thirds of that water is contained in glaciers. Presently, glaciers cover about ten percent of Earth's surface. Glaciers are found only at high elevations and in polar regions such as Greenland and Antarctica. It has been estimated that if all the ice present in the polar regions melted, the level of the oceans would rise about 200 feet!

Rivers form when precipitation that runs off

Earth's surface follows the same path over long periods of time. Small rills join to form creeks. Creeks join to form streams. Streams join to form rivers.

River channels vary in width. Some are less than a few feet wide. The Mississippi River is about one mile wide in some places. Water in a river channel moves the fastest near the center of the channel. All rivers move along their channels to the ultimate base level—the ocean.

Lakes are depressions, or basins, which fill up with water. Most lakes are freshwater lakes. Some lakes in the United States, including the thousands of lakes in Minnesota and the Great Salt Lake in Utah, formed when ancient glaciers melted. Other lakes form when river bends become cut off from the main river. Some lakes form when ground water reaches Earth's surface. Other lakes are made by people.

Water has existed on Earth since its formation 4.5 billion years ago and continues to move throughout the planet and its atmosphere via the water cycle. Perhaps some of the water you drank today may have been used by an ancient Egyptian who labored to build the pyramids 4,600 years ago! ■

Lesson Review

Fill in the circle containing the letter of the term or phrase that correctly completes each statement.

1. The water cycle is powered by energy from the _____.
   (a) moon   (b) planets   (c) sun   (d) all of the above

2. As water vapor rises, it _____.
   (a) cools   (b) condenses   (c) forms water droplets   (d) all of the above

3. _____ are collections of millions of water droplets suspended in air.
   (a) Clouds   (b) Oceans   (c) Lakes   (d) Rivers

4. Most precipitation falls over _____.
   (a) lakes   (b) oceans   (c) land   (d) rivers

5. _____ is the process by which plants add water to the air.
   (a) Evaporation   (b) Condensation   (c) Precipitation   (d) Transpiration

6. Sodium chloride is also known as _____.
   (a) calcium chloride   (b) table salt   (c) table sugar   (d) bromide

7. Most water on Earth is found in _____.
   (a) oceans   (b) rivers   (c) glaciers   (d) none of the above

8. _____ are depressions or basins that fill with fresh water.
   (a) Oceans   (b) Rivers   (c) Glaciers   (d) Lakes

● 9. A river will dump the most eroded material _____.
   (a) at its top   (b) on the sides   (c) in the middle   (d) in the ocean

● 10. It would be easiest to float in a(n) _____ because of its density.
   (a) river   (b) lake   (c) pond   (d) ocean

Lesson 3

Ground Water

People need fresh water for drinking, bathing, doing laundry, and cooking. Fresh water is also needed in agriculture and in many industries. Fortunately, the water that evaporates from the oceans and falls to Earth is fresh water. But less than one percent of Earth's water is available for use, and most of this fresh water is found beneath Earth's surface as **ground water.**

Recall that ground water is water that sinks into Earth's crust. Ground water fills all the open spaces in subsurface sediments and rocks. **Sediments** are unconsolidated particles such as mud, clay, sand, gravel, and pebbles. The amount of ground water depends on the type of subsurface materials. Small sediments, such as clay, have very small spaces among the extremely fine particles. Therefore, clays can hold very limited amounts of water. Coarser sediments such as sand and gravel hold larger amounts of water. Some rocks, such as sandstones, can hold water in the spaces between the sand grains they are made of.

The space occupied by ground water is called the zone of saturation. Rocks and sediments in this zone are saturated, or filled, with water. The upper limit of this zone is the **water table**. The area above the water table is the zone of aeration. Sediments and rocks in this zone are filled mainly with air.

The depth of the water table depends upon the amount of rain that falls in an area and the kind of soil and rocks that underlie the area. At times, the water table may rise to Earth's surface. Swamps form when the water table is at the surface. Lakes occupy areas where the water table is above the surface. Springs, creeks, and some wells are supplied by ground water. People who live over high water tables can usually get fresh water by digging

shallow wells. At times, the water table may fall. During a dry season a shallow well might dry up due to the lowering of the water table.

An **aquifer** is a layer of rock or sediments that can transmit ground water freely. Aquifers are often found between two layers of clay or other materials through which water cannot pass as readily. Aquifers are essential sources of water in many areas and must be protected so that they remain pure and usable.

Aquifers are often tapped by artesian wells. An **artesian well** is a well in which water rises above the level where it was first encountered. If there is enough pressure in the underground source, the water will flow to the surface of an artesian well without the use of pumps. In some artesian wells, however, pumps are needed to bring the water to Earth's surface.

The dam in the upper part of this photograph channels water from rivers into canals that serve farm lands and urban areas.

If precipitation fell evenly throughout the world, all parts of Earth would receive about 26 inches of precipitation each year. But, due to geographical and geological factors, precipitation is distributed unevenly. Mount Waialeale in Hawaii gets an average of about 460 inches a year, while Arica, Chile, once went 14 years without rain. Therefore, freshwater shortages occur in many places because of lack of rain.

Erosion also has decreased the amount of water that becomes ground water. In areas where grasslands have been overgrazed or where forest fires have removed vegetation, much of the soil that absorbs precipitation has been lost. As a result, precipitation tends to run off Earth's surface rather than sinking into the ground. In some places, the water table has been lowered over 100 feet.

Overpopulation also puts a strain on available water supplies. Because much needed fresh water is not always readily available, people have realized the need for water conservation. **Conservation** is the wise and careful use of Earth's resources. Good farming methods, selective cutting of timber, and well-managed grasslands are just a few of the methods used to help conserve Earth's precious resource of fresh water. In what ways can you conserve water?

The quantity of fresh water that is available to people is not the only important factor. Quality also must be considered. Much of the fresh water used by people is stored in reservoirs. A **reservoir** is an artificial lake. When ground water reaches a reservoir, it often contains suspended particles of clay and other sediments. It also contains dissolved particles that can affect its color and taste.

Suspended materials either sink slowly to the bottom of the reservoir or are removed through a sand filter through a process known as **filtration.** To eliminate some of the dissolved particles, chemicals are added to the water. Chlorine is added to kill certain bacteria. Very small amounts of chlorine are needed to treat millions of gallons of water. After the water has been filtered and treated with chemicals, it may be sprayed or trickled through the air to restore its oxygen content in a process called **aeration.** Aeration improves the taste and odor of the water. ■

Lesson Review

In the space provided, write the word or words that best complete each statement.

1. The upper limit of the zone of saturation is the _____.

2. _____ fills all the open spaces in subsurface sediments and rocks.

3. Unconsolidated particles of mud, clay, sand, and gravel are _____.

4. Sediments in the zone of aeration are filled mainly with _____.

5. The wise and careful use of Earth's resources is _____.

6. _____ is used to kill certain bacteria in fresh water.

7. The process of restoring oxygen to water is called _____.

8. _____ removes suspended materials from water.

● 9. Silt is sediment that is finer than sand. Silt will hold _____ water than sand.

● 10. As a source of ground water, gravels are an example of a(n) _____.

Fresh Water in the Future

Earth's human population numbered about 500 million in 1650. By 1850, the human population had doubled. By 1985, it doubled again. By the year 2025, a mere 40 years later, the number of people on Earth is expected to grow four times larger. This rapid increase in the number of humans living on Earth at one time has been called the **population explosion.**

The large increase in the human population in a relatively short period of time increases the demand for Earth's resources. Water is one resource needed by all living things. People need fresh water for personal uses, such as bathing and drinking. Industries use vast amounts of water in manufacturing. Farmers depend on water to raise crops. How will the demands for fresh water be met?

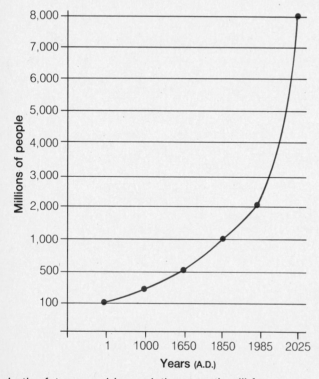

In the future, world population growth will far exceed past growth. The human population growth will increase the demand for fresh water.

Ground water provides most of the fresh water used by homes and industries, and in agriculture. But ground water moves through the water cycle very slowly. The average rate of movement of ground water through Earth's crust is only about 500 feet per year.

In many parts of the United States, ground water has been pumped from wells at a much quicker rate than it is able to be replaced. Often, this results in a significant lowering of the water table. Along some coastal areas, the removal rates have been so much faster than the rate of replacement that denser seawater from the ocean has invaded the freshwater supply.

Another problem that results from extensive pumping of ground water is subsidence, or sinking, of the ground. If too much ground water is removed too quickly from an area, the ground will subside. This problem is most common in areas where thick sediments underlie the surface. When the water is withdrawn, the sediments become compacted, or pressed together, causing the ground above them to sink.

What are some alternatives to using ground water to supply people with fresh water? Earth is sometimes called the "Water Planet." Oceans cover over 139,000,000 square miles of Earth, yet ocean water is unsuitable for almost all uses in homes, in factories, and on farms. The salts in ocean water rust machinery. Ocean water kills crops that are watered with it and kills humans and other animals that drink too much of it.

Salts can be removed from seawater through a process called **desalination**. Desalination can be accomplished by a number of methods. The method most commonly used is distillation. Distillation is a process by which seawater is boiled. The resulting steam is then piped into a cooled container. As the steam rises, the salts are left behind. When the steam comes into contact with the surface of the cooled container, it condenses, providing fresh water suitable for drinking. Distillation is not new. Julius Caesar used this method in Egypt 2,000 years ago to provide drinking water for his soldiers.

Distillation, like all desalination methods, requires large amounts of energy. Therefore, the cost of fresh water produced by desalination is fairly high. Desalination plants aboard ships or located along ocean shores can easily produce and distribute fresh water to passengers or to nearby residents. However, the cost of providing such water to people far from the sea is very high.

Scientists and engineers are currently working to develop power plants that will provide electric power as well as desalinate ocean water. If successful, these dual-purpose plants will lower the costs of desalination.

Another source of fresh water is glaciers. Glaciers cover over ten percent of Earth's land surface. Some scientists have proposed that **icebergs**, large pieces of ice that break off a glacier, be melted to provide people with fresh water. As with desalination, there are problems associated with using icebergs as a source of fresh water. To prevent melting during transport, the icebergs would have to be insulated. The cost of towing the icebergs from the polar regions to areas needing fresh water are also high. Depending upon its size, it could take over a year to tow an iceberg to its destination. Despite these concerns, however, glaciers may be sources of fresh water in the future.

At the present time, these alternative sources of fresh water are very costly. It is therefore every person's responsibility to use Earth's water wisely. What can you do to conserve fresh water? ∎

Lesson Review

Determine whether each of the following statements is true or false. Correct each false statement by crossing out the word or phrase that makes it false and writing the correct word or phrase above it.

_____ 1. From 1650 to 1850, Earth's human population had tripled.

_____ 2. Water is a resource needed by all living things.

_____ 3. Icebergs provide most of Earth's fresh water needs.

_____ 4. Pumping ground water at rates greater than the rate of replacement causes subsidence and sometimes lowers the water table.

_____ 5. Salts in ocean water are valuable to plants and animals.

_____ 6. Desalination is the addition of salts to ocean water.

_____ 7. Presently, distillation is very cheap.

_____ 8. Glaciers are a potential source of fresh water.

• _____ 9. By the year 2025, the estimated number of people on Earth will be about 100 million.

• _____ 10. The average rate of movement of ground water through Earth's crust is about four feet per month.

Water Pollution

The grounding of the Exxon supertanker *Valdez* in 1989 spilled nearly 11 million gallons of crude oil into Alaska's Prince William Sound. But not all water pollution is this obvious. **Water pollution** is the placing of chemicals and wastes into bodies of water that make the water unhealthful. Common pollutants are human and other animal wastes, metals, detergents, dyes, toxic chemicals, and crude oil. Most water pollution can be traced to three sources: industrial wastes, sewage, and agricultural wastes.

Pollutants may make the water unfit for human consumption or use. Animals that drink polluted water are also in danger. The presence of large amounts of pollutants can reduce the amount of oxygen in a body of water. Aquatic life forms depend on oxygen and will die if their supply of this important gas is reduced.

Industrial wastes are chemicals and other substances discarded during or after the manufacturing process. In the United States, industry is the leading cause of water pollution. Factories discharge more than three times as many pollutants as do all sewage systems. Much of the industrial wastes are discharged directly into water systems.

Some industrial pollutants contribute to the formation of acid rain. **Acid rain** forms when certain air pollutants mix with moisture in the atmosphere. Industries that burn coal or oil release nitrogen oxide and sulfur dioxide into the air. When these compounds combine with moisture in the air, they form acids that fall to Earth with rain or snow. Large quantities of acid rain can change the acidity of lakes, ponds, streams, and rivers, thus killing fish and other life forms.

Many industries use water in manufacturing. Often water is used for cooling purposes. If this hot water is discharged into water supplies, thermal pollution may result. Thermal pollution may kill some plants and animals that need cooler water. Thermal pollution also reduces the amount of oxygen in the water, causing the death of many aquatic life forms.

Another major source of water pollution is **sewage**. Sewage is liquid and solid waste that is carried by sewers or drains. Human wastes, chemical wastes, bath water, and laundry water are all forms of sewage. Most sewage goes through treatment plants, but most of these plants do not remove all the other impurities. Water polluted with human or animal wastes contains certain bacteria that can cause deadly diseases if the water is not treated properly. It is estimated that about 11 percent of all sewage in the United States goes into our waters untreated.

Agricultural wastes include fertilizers and pesticides that have been used on crops.

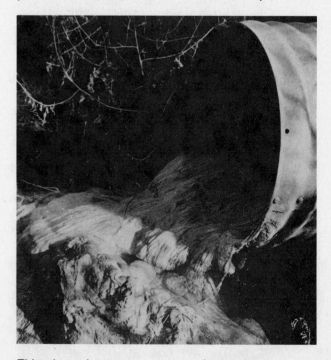

This pipe releases raw sewage into a stream.

Other agricultural wastes are the wastes from farm animals. Rain and snow that run off farmlands wash these substances into lakes and rivers, where they pollute the water.

Water pollution affects the economy, destroys scenic and recreational bodies of water, and harms plants, wildlife, and humans. Water pollution can also be deadly. No one wants to swim in water that smells bad or contains visible pollutants. Nor does anyone want to drink water that contains toxic chemicals and metals. Most industrial wastes poison fish and shellfish and make them unfit for people to eat. Oil spills often kill fish, shorebirds, and mammals that live in or near the polluted water.

What can be done about water pollution problems? Stricter regulations can be imposed on industries requiring them to treat wastes before discharging them into Earth's waters. Sewage must be thoroughly treated before it is discharged. Limiting the use of pesticides and fertilizers will reduce not only water pollution but air pollution as well. The Safe Drinking Water Act was designed by the federal government to protect water supplies from pollution. The Environmental Protection Agency (EPA) is a government agency that regulates, among other things, the amounts of bacteria, chemicals, and metals in water supplies.

Eliminating water pollution will require tough laws and money. People are beginning to realize that although we inhabit the "Water Planet," water is a valuable commodity that must not be wasted. The alternative can be even more costly. ■

Lesson Review

In the space before each number, write the letter of the word or group of words in Column 2 that matches the description in Column 1.

Column 1

_____ 1. the introduction of any substances that make a body of water unhealthful

_____ 2. dyes, metals, toxic chemicals, detergents, human and animal wastes

_____ 3. gas important to aquatic life forms

_____ 4. leading cause of water pollution in the United States

_____ 5. forms when nitrogen oxide and sulfur dioxide combine with moisture in the air

_____ 6. occurs when hot water is discharged into a body of water

_____ 7. solid and liquid wastes carried in drains and sewers

_____ 8. fertilizers and pesticides

● _____ 9. one solution to thermal pollution

● _____ 10. possible solution to pollution by agriculture

Column 2

a. acid rain

b. agricultural wastes

c. cooling towers

d. industrial wastes

e. organic farming

f. oxygen

g. pollutants

h. sewage

i. thermal pollution

j. water pollution

Foresters specialize in the management of forests, which play an important role in water conservation.

Hydrologists are scientists who study Earth's water cycle. Some hydrologists locate new sources of fresh water. They assist in finding the best places to drill wells in areas that are in need of fresh water. These scientists also identify areas that are in danger of flooding and aid in the development of flood prevention plans. Hydrologists often work for state and local governments and in industries that supply water. Hydrologists locate aquifers, determine their capacities, and make recommendations to protect freshwater sources from pollution.

Oceanographers are geologists who study the oceans, the largest bodies of water on Earth. Some oceanographers study ocean waves, currents, and tides. Others concentrate on the chemical makeup of sea water. Some oceanographers focus on the features of the ocean floor and determine how these features were formed. One group of oceanographers studies the organisms found in the world's oceans and the ways in which changes in the ocean environment affect them. These oceanographers also look for ways to increase the amount of food taken from the oceans. Current research suggests that four or five times as much food from the sea is available than is currently harvested.

Foresters are scientists who specialize in the management of forests. Properly maintained forests not only provide a supply of lumber, but they also play an important role in water conservation. Almost all forests are watersheds that supply rivers and streams with much of their water. Foresters see to it that forest soil is kept in place by planting trees and shrubs in open forest areas. Forests must also maintain a good cover of grass in areas where animals feed. These measures prevent too much water from flowing over the soil and carrying it into rivers and streams.

Chemists are scientists who study matter and its properties. Water is a unique form of matter. Some chemists work in phases of water management. These scientists help to design and operate water treatment plants. They often analyze the composition of water and, if necessary, develop programs to maintain pure water. Chemists also work to restore bodies of water that have become polluted. Many chemists are employed by government agencies that have the legal responsibility to maintain clean water.

In the field of water control and water quality, there are a number of career opportunities for technicians of various kinds. These people work closely with scientists in the gathering and testing of samples. Opportunities for assistants also exist in laboratories that analyze and monitor water quality. State and federal agencies employ many workers who keep forest lands properly planted and protected. The battle to maintain clean water has also created a number of opportunities in the enforcement area. Government agencies employ investigators and inspectors who see to it that laws and regulations are observed. ∎

For Further Information

More information about these and related careers is available from the following publications and organizations.

Careers in Engineering and Technology, George C. Beakley, Macmillan, 1987

Careers in Chemistry: Questions and Answers, American Chemical Society, 1982

Ocean Frontiers, Eryl Davis, Viking, 1980

Your Future in Forestry, David H. Hanaburgh, Richards Rosen, 1979

American Chemical Society
1155 16th Street
Washington, DC 20036

American Geological Institute
5205 Leesburg Pike
Falls Church, VA 22041

American Forestry Association
1319 18th Street
Washington, DC 20036

Air

Earth is surrounded by a blanket of air called the atmosphere.

Lesson 1

The Atmosphere

Earth is surrounded by a blanket of air that stretches hundreds of miles above its surface. This air is called the atmosphere. Earth's **atmosphere** protects Earth and those who live on it.

Many biological processes depend on air. Earth's atmosphere screens out some of the harmful radiation from the sun. If it weren't for the atmosphere, many meteoroids would reach Earth's surface, marking it with craters.

Earth's atmosphere contains many gases. **Nitrogen**, N_2, is the most abundant gas in our atmosphere. About 78 percent of Earth's air is made of nitrogen. Nitrogen is important to most living things, but few living things can use nitrogen directly from the air. Bacteria change nitrogen into a form that is usable.

Oxygen, O_2, makes up about 21 percent of the air that surrounds us. Trees and green plants produce oxygen as they make food.

Animals, including humans, use oxygen directly from the air or dissolved in water.

Other gases are found in our atmosphere, but they only make up about one percent of its contents. Carbon dioxide, CO_2, is essential to plant life. Plants use it to make food. Plants take in carbon dioxide and, in turn, produce oxygen. Humans inhale oxygen and produce carbon dioxide when they exhale.

Gases near Earth's surface are closer together due to the pressure of the air above them. Thus, air near Earth's surface is more dense than air at higher levels.

Earth's atmosphere has four layers. The layer nearest Earth is the **troposphere**. Clouds occupy the troposphere, and almost all weather takes place in this layer. Temperatures in this layer generally decrease about 3.5°F with every 1,000-foot increase in altitude.

The **stratosphere** begins about ten miles above Earth and extends upward to about

30 miles. The air is dry and clouds are rare. Aircraft use the lower part of the stratosphere to avoid the weather below. Ozone is found in the upper part of the stratosphere. **Ozone** is a form of oxygen that absorbs most of the dangerous ultraviolet rays of the sun.

The layer of air above the stratosphere is the **mesosphere**. This is the coldest part of the atmosphere. The temperature can drop to as low as 150° below zero. The mesosphere ends about 50 miles above Earth.

The outermost layer of Earth's atmosphere is called the **thermosphere**. Its lower section is the **ionosphere**. Temperatures in this layer range from about 1,100°F to 3,600°F! The ionosphere is made of electrically charged particles, which play a role in long-distance radio communication. The particles reflect, or bounce, radio waves back to Earth.

The upper section of the thermosphere is the **exosphere**. It begins about 300 miles above Earth. Its density is so low that Earth-orbiting spacecraft encounter almost no resistance. The exosphere extends into interplanetary space about 600 miles above Earth. ■

Lesson Review

Fill in the circle containing the letter of the term or phrase that correctly completes each statement.

1. Earth's atmosphere _____.
   - ⓐ is important to many biological processes
   - ⓑ protects Earth from harmful radiation
   - ⓒ shields Earth from meteoroids
   - ⓓ all of the above

2. The most abundant gas in Earth's atmosphere is _____.
   - ⓐ nitrogen
   - ⓑ oxygen
   - ⓒ carbon dioxide
   - ⓓ ozone

3. Plants use _____ to make food.
   - ⓐ nitrogen
   - ⓑ oxygen
   - ⓒ carbon dioxide
   - ⓓ ozone

4. The layer of air closest to Earth is the _____.
   - ⓐ exosphere
   - ⓑ ionosphere
   - ⓒ troposphere
   - ⓓ stratosphere

5. To escape storms, commercial aircraft often fly in the _____.
   - ⓐ troposphere
   - ⓑ stratosphere
   - ⓒ ionosphere
   - ⓓ mesosphere

6. The coldest part of the atmosphere is the _____.
   - ⓐ mesosphere
   - ⓑ ionosphere
   - ⓒ stratosphere
   - ⓓ exosphere

7. _____ absorbs most of the ultraviolet radiation from the sun.
   - ⓐ Carbon dioxide
   - ⓑ Nitrogen
   - ⓒ Ozone
   - ⓓ None of the above

8. The _____ is made of electrically charged particles.
   - ⓐ troposphere
   - ⓑ mesosphere
   - ⓒ ionosphere
   - ⓓ stratosphere

● 9. The layer of Earth's atmosphere in which thunderstorms would occur is the _____.
   - ⓐ troposphere
   - ⓑ exosphere
   - ⓒ ionosphere
   - ⓓ mesosphere

● 10. Atmospheric pressure measures the density of air. The pressure would be greatest _____.
   - ⓐ in the troposphere
   - ⓑ in the exosphere
   - ⓒ in the ionosphere
   - ⓓ in the mesosphere

Weather and Climate

Weather is the state or condition of the atmosphere at any given time and place. Weather can last for several days. Or, it can last for only a few minutes. Weather influences the way people dress, and it sometimes determines their outdoor activities. It also affects crop growth. Bad weather can snarl transportation, close schools and businesses, affect the prices of food, and sometimes disrupt everyday living. Good weather, on the other hand, tends to keep these activities routine.

Recall that although some weather may reach up into the lower parts of the stratosphere, most occurs in the troposphere, the lowest level of Earth's atmosphere. Weather is caused by interactions among air, water, and solar energy. Weather that occurs in the troposphere primarily depends on four factors: temperature, air pressure, wind, and moisture.

Temperature is a measure of the hotness or coldness of a body, or the amount of internal energy it contains. Of all the incoming energy from the sun, 30 percent is scattered back into the air. About 20 percent is absorbed by clouds and the atmosphere and never reaches Earth's surface. The remaining 50 percent of the sun's energy is absorbed by Earth's surface. It is this portion of solar energy that is returned to the atmosphere as heat. Carbon dioxide and water vapor in the air absorb this energy and keep heat in the troposphere. This warming of Earth's atmosphere is similar to what happens in a greenhouse. A greenhouse lets sunlight in to warm the plants. The glass or plastic from which the greenhouse is built prevents the heat from escaping.

Because it is matter, air has mass and takes up space. **Air pressure** is a force per unit area of air that pushes against Earth's

Weather is the state of the atmosphere at any given time and place.

surface. Near Earth's surface, the particles that make up air are closer together because of the pressure of the overlying particles of air. Air becomes less dense with an increase in elevation.

Air pressure also is related to the temperature of air. Warm air is less dense than cool air and therefore pushes against Earth's surface with less force than cool air. Because it is less dense, warm air tends to rise, creating a low pressure area. Clouds and stormy weather usually occur with low-pressure areas.

On the other hand, cool air is more dense than warm air and tends to sink, creating a high-pressure area. Inside a high-pressure area, the skies are usually clear. Near the margins of a high-pressure area, precipitation and clouds are common.

A **barometer** is an instrument that measures air pressure. When the barometer is said to be rising, air pressure is increasing, and the chances of having better weather are improving. When the barometer is said to be falling, air pressure is decreasing, and the chances of having poor weather are likely.

Wind is air in motion. Winds transport moisture and heat from one place to another. The velocity of a wind is due to the fact that less-densely packed air particles in higher elevations will travel at higher speeds than those in lower elevations.

Moisture in the atmosphere is called **humidity.** Warm air particles are farther apart from one another than cool air particles. Therefore, a certain volume of warm air is able to hold more moisture in the form of water vapor than the same volume of cool air. When a volume of air cools and can no longer hold its water vapor, the water vapor condenses. The temperature at which condensation occurs is the **dew point.** The dew that covers the grass and leaves on some mornings is the result of condensation of water vapor in the air. If the air temperature is below freezing, the water vapor will form frost.

How does weather differ from climate? **Climate** is the average weather conditions of an area over several decades. Climates can be classified into three zones based on the amount of solar energy received by a certain area of Earth. The **tropical zone** is the area between $23\frac{1}{2}°$ north and south latitudes. Temperatures in the tropics are very hot, except at high elevations. The **polar zones** extend from each pole to $66\frac{1}{2}°$ north and south latitudes. Polar regions are always very cold. The **temperate zones** lie between the polar zones and the tropics. Temperate zones have four seasons. In general, winters are cold and summers are hot. Temperatures in autumn and spring are generally mild. ■

Lesson Review

In the space before each number, write the letter of the word or group of words in Column 2 that matches the description in Column 1.

Column 1	Column 2
_____ 1. the state or condition of the atmosphere at any given time or place	a. air pressure
_____ 2. layer of atmosphere where most weather occurs	b. carbon dioxide
_____ 3. the amount of internal energy of a body	c. climate
_____ 4. a gas that keeps heat in the troposphere	d. humidity
_____ 5. force per unit area of air that pushes against Earth's surface	e. low-pressure area
_____ 6. air in motion	f. temperate
_____ 7. moisture in the atmosphere	g. temperature
_____ 8. average of all weather conditions over several decades	h. troposphere
• _____ 9. the climate zone in which the United States is located	i. weather
• _____ 10. type of area in which thunderstorms would be usual	j. wind

Clouds and Precipitation

Clouds play a very important role in Earth's water cycle. Clouds are suspended in the air above Earth's surface. Clouds form when water vapor from bodies of water rises into the air, expands, and cools. As the water vapor cools, it condenses into drops of water or crystals of ice or both and forms clouds.

Almost everything about a cloud offers clues about the weather and how it may change in the near future. A cloud's shape, color, size, height, and velocity tell something about the weather that will arrive soon.

Cirrus clouds are thin, wispy clouds that often resemble strands of hair. The base of a cirrus cloud is over 23,000 feet above Earth. The top of a cirrus cloud can reach 30,000 feet. Cirrus clouds are made of ice crystals. Cirrus clouds do not produce precipitation, but their appearance usually means that stormy weather may be approaching.

Cumulus clouds are thick, puffy clouds with flat bases. Cumulus clouds form between 6,000 and 20,000 feet above Earth. Cumulus clouds can stretch across the sky as white or gray patches. Sometimes these patches form a continuous cloud. Cumulus clouds contain drops of water, ice crystals, or both and often produce precipitation. When they do, they are referred to as cumulonimbus clouds. "Thunderheads" are cumulus clouds that produce drenching rain, lightning, and thunder.

Clouds nearest Earth's surface are **stratus clouds.** Their bases are usually at altitudes of less than 6,000 feet. Stratus clouds are usually dull gray in color and often occur in layers. Nimbostratus clouds generally produce rain or snow and cover the entire sky.

Rain can develop in cumulus and stratus clouds when the air temperature in the clouds is above freezing. Air currents within clouds cause water droplets to be tossed about, to collide, and to grow in size. Eventually, drops become so large that they fall from the cloud as rain. If the temperature in the cloud is below freezing, some ice crystals also will form as water evaporates and freezes. The ice crystals fall from the cloud as snow. The snow will become rain, however, if the temperature outside the cloud is above freezing. Precipitation from a cloud may reach Earth as **sleet** if the precipitation freezes en route to the ground.

Hail is ice that falls from cumulonimbus

Cirrus clouds often have a feathery appearance.

Cumulus clouds are large and billowy.

clouds. Hail forms when water freezes around small pieces of ice. Pieces grow larger as they are tossed between high and low levels of the cloud. Temperatures in the low level are above freezing; in the high level, they are below freezing. As the crystals are tossed up and down, they alternately freeze and melt. Hailstones become too large to be held by the air currents and fall to Earth as balls of ice.

The amount of precipitation produced by clouds varies greatly throughout the world. Some places on Earth receive a great deal of precipitation while others receive very little. Some places near the equator receive over 400 inches of rain per year. Desert areas receive less than ten inches annually.

Snow is less common than rain. Snow falls in the polar regions all year, but less than ten inches accumulates annually. In fact, the heaviest snowfalls occur in winter in the mountains of the temperate zones. ■

Lesson Review

Fill in the circle containing the letter of the term or phrase that correctly completes each statement.

1. Clouds are _____.
   - ⓐ collections of water drops, ice, or both
   - ⓑ suspended in air
   - ⓒ clues to weather
   - ⓓ all of the above

2. _____ are thin, wispy clouds made of ice.
   - ⓐ Cumulus
   - ⓑ Cirrus
   - ⓒ Nimbus
   - ⓓ Stratus

3. Thick, puffy clouds that form between 6,000 and 20,000 feet above Earth's surface are _____ clouds.
   - ⓐ cirrus
   - ⓑ cumulus
   - ⓒ stratus
   - ⓓ nimbus

4. "Thunderheads" are _____ clouds.
   - ⓐ cirrus
   - ⓑ cumulus
   - ⓒ stratus
   - ⓓ all of the above

5. _____ forms in cumulus and stratus clouds when air temperature is above freezing.
   - ⓐ Rain
   - ⓑ Snow
   - ⓒ Hail
   - ⓓ Sleet

6. Precipitation that freezes en route to the ground is _____.
   - ⓐ rain
   - ⓑ snow
   - ⓒ hail
   - ⓓ sleet

7. _____ forms as pieces of ice are tossed up and down in cumulonimbus clouds.
   - ⓐ Rain
   - ⓑ Snow
   - ⓒ Hail
   - ⓓ Sleet

8. Regions near the equator receive about _____ inches of rain per year.
   - ⓐ 4
   - ⓑ 40
   - ⓒ 400
   - ⓓ 4,000

● 9. If it were a gray, overcast day with rain, _____ clouds would probably be overhead.
   - ⓐ cirrus
   - ⓑ nimbostratus
   - ⓒ cirrocumulus
   - ⓓ cirrostratus

● 10. Fog is a _____ cloud.
   - ⓐ cirrus
   - ⓑ cumulus
   - ⓒ stratus
   - ⓓ nimbus

Wind is moving air. Sometimes wind blows so gently that it is barely noticeable. At other times, wind is so powerful that seemingly permanent objects, such as houses and large trees, are torn from the ground.

Weather vanes are used to determine wind direction. Winds are named after the direction from which they come. For example, air moving from the northeast to the southwest is a northeast wind.

An instrument called an anemometer measures wind speed. An anemometer is made of several cups that rotate around a shaft. As wind pushes against the cups, the shaft turns. The number of turns in a certain amount of time is used to determine wind speed.

What causes wind? Earth's major wind patterns are controlled by two factors: the unequal heating of Earth by the sun, and Earth's rotation on its axis. In general, cool air in the polar regions sinks and moves toward the equator. Due to Earth's rotation, warm air near the equator rises and moves toward Earth's poles. This circulation, or movement of air, produces Earth's major wind patterns.

The **trade winds** flow between the equator and the tropics. In the Northern Hemisphere, the trade winds blow from northeast to southwest. In the Southern Hemisphere, they blow from the southeast to the northwest. The trade winds were named by sailors who once relied upon them to move their trade ships between Europe and the Americas.

The **prevailing westerlies** are the major wind system between 30° north and 60° north latitudes and 30° south and 60° south latitudes. In the Northern Hemisphere, the prevailing westerlies blow from the southwest to the northeast. In what direction do they blow in the Southern Hemisphere? The prevailing westerlies move weather systems across the United States and Canada.

Between the poles and 60° north and south latitudes, the **polar easterlies** blow. In the Northern Hemisphere, these winds blow from the northeast to the southwest. In the

Land and sea breezes occur because of temperature differences in the air over land and water.

Southern Hemisphere, they blow from the southeast to the northwest.

In addition to the major wind systems, small-scale circulation is found near Earth's surface. A **sea breeze** forms when cool air over a large body of water flows inland and causes the warm air over the land to rise. Sea breezes are common during the day. At night, cool air over a landmass blows toward a body of water and forces the warm air over the water to rise. This is called a **land breeze.**

Wind is often a feature of most types of severe weather. A **hurricane** is a tropical storm that forms over an ocean. They develop when inflowing air forces moist, warm air over the ocean to rise. A low-pressure area called the eye forms near the center of the storm. Wind speeds during a hurricane can range from about 120 to over 150 miles per hour. Much of the damage is caused by the violent winds and the huge waves caused by these winds.

A **tornado** is a wind storm that moves in a narrow path over land. Tornadoes are narrow, funnel-shaped clouds that form at the base of cumulonimbus clouds. Scientists estimate that wind speeds of tornadoes range from 100 to 250 miles per hour.

Thunderstorms are severe storms that form when masses of warm air rapidly invade masses of cool air. Thunderstorms are often accompanied by winds over 40 miles per hour.

A **blizzard** is a snowstorm that combines temperatures of 10°F with wind speeds of at least 35 miles per hour. Winds blow snow about, often creating deep drifts. Wind-chill factors are usually reported during a blizzard. The wind-chill factor is an energy value that can be converted to an equivalent temperature. For example, if the air temperature is 10°F and the wind is blowing at 20 miles per hour, the wind chill is equivalent to −25°F. ■

Lesson Review

Determine whether each of the following statements is true or false. Correct each false statement by crossing out the word or phrase that makes it false and writing the correct word or phase above it.

_____ 1. Weather vanes use turning cups to measure wind speed.

_____ 2. Due to Earth's rotation, warm air near the equator rises and moves toward the poles.

_____ 3. The trade winds flow between the poles and the tropics.

_____ 4. In the Northern Hemisphere, the prevailing westerlies blow southwest to northeast.

_____ 5. A sea breeze forms when cool air over a landmass flows inland and forces the warm air over the land to rise.

_____ 6. A hurricane develops over land.

_____ 7. Tornadoes are narrow, funnel-shaped storms that move over land.

_____ 8. Winds associated with thunderstorms can exceed 40 miles per hour.

• _____ 9. A wind coming from the north is called a northern wind.

• _____ 10. In the Southern Hemisphere, the prevailing westerlies flow from northwest to southeast.

Forecasting Weather

Meteorology, the science of forecasting the weather, is a young science. However, the desire to know what the weather will be is as old as the human race.

Meteorologists who forecast the weather depend on the collection of weather information. This information is furnished four times each day by more than 3,500 observation stations around the world. These stations record and send information on air temperature, air pressure, wind direction and speed, the amount of moisture in the air, and the amount of precipitation that has fallen.

In addition to these observation stations, about 800 other stations around the world release weather balloons twice each day. Weather balloons carry instruments that measure conditions in the upper atmosphere. Information is also gathered by various aircraft and by weather ships. Finally, satellites equipped with television cameras orbit Earth and transmit pictures from space at regular intervals.

The data that forecasters receive from these sources must be put into a form that will allow forecasts to be made. To do this, forecasters use charts called weather maps. A **weather map** is an outline map of an area. Black circles on weather maps mark observation stations. Around these circles, forecasters use symbols to show all important information from that station's latest report.

The information is added to the map and analyzed. The forecaster begins the analysis by drawing isobars on the map. **Isobars** are lines that connect points that have the same barometric pressure. The isobars help the forecaster to determine the position of fronts.

Fronts are boundaries between air masses with different properties. Fronts are usually

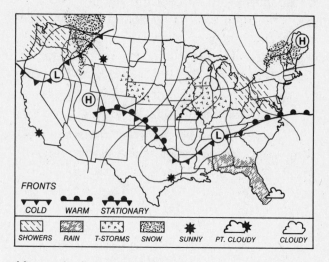

Meteorologists use maps like this one to forecast the weather.

hundreds of miles long and extend upward into the troposphere. In the United States, fronts generally move from west to east. **Warm fronts** develop when a warm air mass moves in to replace a cold air mass. A **cold front** forms when a cold air mass moves in to replace a warm air mass. **Stationary fronts** develop when either a warm front or a cold front stops advancing.

A **low-pressure system** is an area of low pressure that forms between a warm front and a cold front. It is shown on a weather map by a capital "L." Lows produce storms. The severity of the storms depends on how low the pressure is. A low-pressure system is shown on a weather map as a set of closed, curved isobars drawn closely together. A low forms along a cold front that is trailing a warmer air mass.

When two cold air masses join and force the warmer air between them aloft, an **occluded front** forms. The weather associated with an occluded front includes thick strato-cumulus clouds and heavy rain or snow.

A **ridge of high pressure** is a belt that brings sunny skies and pleasant weather. Its center is designated with a capital "H" on a weather map. Ridges of high pressure often form between two low-pressure systems and move with them. When high-pressure areas follow this pattern, they provide a period of fair weather between two unsettled periods.

Forecasters also rely on other forms of information in making their forecasts. They use temperature charts, precipitation charts, information about the force and direction of winds in the upper atmosphere, radar scans, and various other computer-prepared studies. They also rely upon their past experience with the area for which they forecast.

In spite of the wealth of information available, forecasts for even the next 18 to 36 hours are sometimes incorrect. This happens because there are numerous weather conditions that can develop, and they can develop very rapidly. Also, there are simply not enough observation stations available, especially over the oceans, which cover three fourths of Earth's surface. ■

Lesson Review

Fill in the circle containing the letter of the term or phrase that correctly completes each statement.

1. _____ are boundaries between air masses with different properties.
   - (a) Lows
   - (b) Fronts
   - (c) Depressions
   - (d) Isobars

2. Weather data are reported by _____ four times a day.
   - (a) satellites
   - (b) balloons
   - (c) observation stations
   - (d) aircraft

3. A(n) _____ front forms when a warm air mass moves in to replace a cold air mass.
   - (a) warm
   - (b) stationary
   - (c) cold
   - (d) occluded

4. A _____ is an area of low pressure that forms between a warm front and a cold front.
   - (a) ridge
   - (b) high
   - (c) forecast
   - (d) low-pressure system

5. _____ are lines on weather maps that connect points with the same barometric pressure.
   - (a) Fronts
   - (b) Isobars
   - (c) Depressions
   - (d) Parallels

6. A(n) _____ front forms when a cold air mass moves in to replace a warm air mass.
   - (a) cold
   - (b) warm
   - (c) occluded
   - (d) stationary

7. A(n) _____ front forms when two cold air masses merge and force warm air aloft.
   - (a) occluded
   - (b) cold
   - (c) warm
   - (d) stationary

8. Above all, weather forecasting still depends upon _____.
   - (a) experience
   - (b) satellites
   - (c) collected information
   - (d) all of the above

● 9. A location near an "H" on a weather map is likely to have _____ weather.
   - (a) fair
   - (b) rainy
   - (c) freezing
   - (d) unsettled

● 10. Today's weather in Chicago is likely to reach _____ in a day or two.
   - (a) Dallas
   - (b) San Francisco
   - (c) Denver
   - (d) New York

Air Pollution

In many cities around the world, a blanket of "haze" often forms when winds are calm. This "haze" sometimes becomes so thick that it blocks the sun's light. What would otherwise be a sunny day becomes dull and overcast.

On "hazy" days, people in these cities are often troubled by burning eyes, nose and throat irritations, and the sharp smell of chemicals. These people are suffering from air pollution. **Air pollution** is the addition of harmful amounts of certain gases, chemicals, and tiny particles of solid matter to the air.

What are the sources of air pollution? Some air pollution is the result of common Earth processes. Volcanoes and natural fires add dust, soot, ash, and gases to Earth's atmosphere. Most air pollution, however, is the result of human activities. Cars, buses, trains, motorcycles, planes, trucks, cigarettes, fires, construction, and mining add pollutants to the air.

The various forms of transportation are major contributors to air pollution. Exhaust from motor vehicles, trains, ships, and planes releases harmful amounts of gases and chemical compounds called **hydrocarbons** into the air. The release of harmful gases into the air by motor vehicles has been reduced by catalytic converters. **Catalytic converters** are devices that recirculate the harmful gases for more complete burning before releasing them.

Smog is a common air pollutant. **Smog** is a combination of smoke, certain gases, and fog. There are two kinds of smog. Sulfurous smog is a gray smog that forms when coal, oil, and natural gas are burned. When they are burned, they release sulfur dioxide and dust into the air. Photochemical smog forms when nitric oxide, sulfur dioxide, and hydrocarbons combine to produce a brownish-yellow smog.

The manufacturing processes of many factories are also major contributors to air pollution. Many plants produce large amounts of harmful gases and particulates, or small particles of solid matter, which are released into the air. To control pollution, filter systems that remove impurities have been placed in many smoke-stacks. Strict laws now regulate the types of fuels used in factories. These laws restrict the amounts of pollutants that can be released into Earth's atmosphere.

What does air pollution do to people? People who breathe polluted air may have eye, nose, and throat irritation. Some studies also have found a strong link between air pollution and certain kinds of cancer in humans.

Many cities issue daily reports on the quality of air. Based on the Pollution Standard Index, air quality is classified as *good, moderate,* or *unhealthful.* The unhealthful category may be further subdivided into *alert, warning,* and *emergency* conditions. An emergency condition signals danger to people who have problems that involve the lungs or the heart.

In addition to health problems connected with air pollution, there is great concern about how air pollution affects the ozone layer. This layer of gas is about 15 miles above Earth. Recall that ozone is a form of oxygen that screens out the ultraviolet rays of the sun. Ultraviolet rays are harmful to living tissue. Without the ozone layer, many scientists believe that life on Earth would be impossible.

The ozone layer is threatened by the use of chlorofluorocarbons (CFCs). CFCs are gases that break down molecules of ozone. Damage to the ozone layer will allow more ultraviolet radiation to reach Earth. This would cause an increase in skin cancer and may produce a global warming effect. The use of CFCs in aerosol cans has been banned. However, CFCs are still used in air conditioners and refrigerators, and in many packing foams.

How does air pollution affect other organisms? Recall that acid rain is precipitation that forms when certain air pollutants mix with moisture in the atmosphere. Acid rain has affected forests in Europe and North America. It also has polluted bodies of water and caused the death of aquatic life.

Despite the efforts to reduce it, air pollution is still a major environmental concern. During the past 30 years, the problem has gotten worse because of the rapid growth of the human population and the accompanying growth of industry. Not only does air pollution threaten our planet, but current estimates are that air pollution problems in the United States alone cost about $20 billion per year. ■

To reduce air pollution, many factories are installing filters in smokestacks.

Lesson Review

Determine whether each of the following statements is true or false. Correct each false statement by crossing out the word or phrase that makes it false and writing the correct word or phrase above it.

_____ 1. Air pollution is the addition of harmful amounts of certain gases, chemicals, and solid matter to the air.

_____ 2. Most air pollution is the result of natural causes.

_____ 3. Exhaust from cars and other motor vehicles gives off hydrocarbons.

_____ 4. Sulfurous smog forms when sulfur dioxide and dust are released into the air.

_____ 5. Catalytic converters are devices that recirculate harmful gases in motor vehicles before releasing the gases into the air.

_____ 6. The ozone layer doesn't screen out ultraviolet rays from the sun.

_____ 7. CFCs break down ozone molecules.

_____ 8. CFCs are still used in aerosol cans.

● _____ 9. Farming areas probably have more air pollution than nearby cities.

● _____ 10. Damage to the ozone layer could cause polar ice sheets to melt and cause the level of the oceans to rise.

Many environmental engineers develop and monitor equipment that measures air pollution.

Meteorologists are scientists who collect information on the condition of the atmosphere in a particular area at a particular time. This information is then transferred to maps that are used for short-range and long-range weather forecasting. Many meteorologists work for the National Weather Service, which is part of the National Oceanic and Atmospheric Administration. Most of these meteorologists staff the almost 300 weather stations that are located throughout the United States. A few meteorologists report the weather for local news stations.

Climatologists study Earth's atmosphere over an extended period of time. They gather and examine long range information on the temperature, humidity, wind speed and direction, amount of sunshine, and precipitation of an area in order to describe the area's climate. Climatologists often do research at colleges and universities, but some are employed by the National Weather Service. Some climatologists work for companies that have an interest in agriculture. These scientists work with others toward the further development of agriculture in various parts of the world.

Environmental engineers work to control and prevent various kinds of pollution. Many work in the area of air pollution. These engineers develop equipment that measures air pollution, and, in turn, they design air pollution control devices. Many environmental engineers work for private companies that manufacture such equipment. Some engineers are employed by a federal agency called the EPA, or the Environmental Protection Agency. Others work for similar agencies on the state level. Environmental engineers develop standards that private industry must meet to reduce or stop pollution. They also conduct inspections and help to administer enforcement programs.

Aerodynamic engineers study the forces that act on an object moving through air. Aerodynamic engineers use their knowledge of these forces to design aircraft and other flying objects. A knowledge of aerodynamics is also essential for the proper design of a variety of structures and vehicles. Aerodynamic engineers work with architects to design skyscrapers that can withstand high winds. They work with automobile designers to produce cars and trucks that are properly streamlined. Aerodynamic engineers work for companies that build engines, aircraft, and boats. Many work for such federal agencies as the National Aeronautics and Space Administration and the Federal Aviation Administration.

Job opportunities exist for many professionals and technicians at weather stations throughout the country. These facilities employ observers who gather and transmit essential information daily. Opportunities also exist in the growing field of air pollution control. Agencies that monitor and enforce air pollution control standards employ field inspectors and various kinds of technicians. The EPA employs many people who are active in the area of enforcement of antipollution programs. ∎

For Further Information

More information about these and related careers is available from the following publications and organizations.

The Weather Book, Ralph Hardy, Little, Brown, 1982

What's Happening to Our Climate?, Malcolm Weiss, Simon & Schuster, 1978

Your Future in Aeronautic Engineering, Richards Rosen, 1978

American Meteorological Society
45 Beacon Street
Boston, MA 02108

American Institute of Aeronautics and
 Astronautics
1633 Broadway
New York, NY 10019

Plants

Plants of all sizes and shapes grow almost everywhere on Earth.

Characteristics of Plants

How are you like elephants and roses? Humans, other animals, and plants are living things. The study of living things is **biology**.

Most biologists classify, or group, living things into five kingdoms. Bacteria belong to the moneran kingdom. Mushrooms are grouped in the fungus kingdom. Some kinds of algae are members of the protist kingdom. Mosses, other kinds of algae, trees, and flowers belong to the plant kingdom. Worms, fish, people, and many other kinds of animals belong to the animal kingdom.

Although they belong to different kingdoms, all living things are alike in some ways. All living things are made of cells. **Cells** are the building blocks of life. Cells carry out many of the functions of living things. All living things grow and reproduce because of cells.

All cells have a cell membrane, cytoplasm, and material that controls the life of the cell. A **cell membrane** is a thin layer of proteins and fats that holds the different parts of the cell together. **Cytoplasm** is a jellylike substance that contains many cell materials such as proteins, waste products, and dissolved minerals.

Living things are also very different from one another. Plant cells differ from animal cells in several ways. Plant cells have a **cell wall**, a rigid layer that shapes and supports a plant cell. Cellulose is present in plant cell walls. Cellulose strengthens the roots, stems, and leaves of many plants. Most plants contain a green substance called **chlorophyll**. Plants use chlorophyll to make food.

Plants and animals are different in other ways, too. Most animals are mobile; they can move. Most plants are stationary or immobile; they cannot move from place to place. Plants are able to make their own food. Animals must rely on plants or other animals for food.

Botanists, scientists who study plants, have classified over 275,000 species of plants. A **species** is a subgroup of organisms in a kingdom whose members are able to reproduce. Plant species vary in size from the giant redwoods to tiny orchids. Each species occupies its own **habitat,** or place in which it naturally lives. The habitat of most cacti is Earth's deserts. Palms live in tropical habitats.

Most species of plants have roots, stems, and leaves. Roots anchor plants in the ground. Roots absorb water and other nutrients from the soil. Certain tissues then carry the water and nutrients to other parts of the plant. Stems support a plant's leaves. Nutrients are carried to different parts of the plant through the stem. Some stems also store food. Leaves are the parts that trap light and make food for the plant.

Plants are one of the most important resources on Earth. Plants provide food in the form of fruits and vegetables. Plants are food for some of the animals that we eat. Wood for building comes from plants. Coal is the fossilized remains of plants. Cork, rubber, and turpentine come from plants. Certain textiles, such as cotton and rayon, are made from plant fibers. Plants also provide us with many medicines. ■

Lesson Review

Fill in the circle containing the letter of the term or phrase that correctly completes each statement.

1. _____ is the study of all living things.
   ⓐ Botany   ⓑ Cytoplasm   ⓒ Biology   ⓓ Species

2. In the five kingdom classification, mushrooms belong to the _____ kingdom.
   ⓐ plant   ⓑ animal   ⓒ fungus   ⓓ protist

3. All living things are made of _____.
   ⓐ algae   ⓑ cells   ⓒ fungus   ⓓ stems

4. _____ is the jellylike substance of a cell that contains proteins, waste and minerals.
   ⓐ Cytoplasm   ⓑ Chlorophyll   ⓒ Cell wall   ⓓ Membrane

5. Plants use _____ to make food.
   ⓐ stems   ⓑ chlorophyll   ⓒ cellulose   ⓓ minerals

6. A _____ is a group of organisms whose members are able to reproduce.
   ⓐ habitat   ⓑ cell   ⓒ species   ⓓ kingdom

7. _____ anchor most plants to the ground.
   ⓐ Stems   ⓑ Leaves   ⓒ Cells   ⓓ Roots

8. _____ make food for the plant.
   ⓐ Roots   ⓑ Stems   ⓒ Leaves   ⓓ Protists

● 9. Most plants need light to make chlorophyll. If a plant has no light, its leaves will _____.
   ⓐ stay very green   ⓑ lose color   ⓒ grow   ⓓ none of the above

● 10. A cactus plant will grow best in _____.
   ⓐ a polar region   ⓑ the tropics   ⓒ a desert   ⓓ a swamp area

Photosynthesis and Respiration

Recall that most plants have roots, stems, and leaves. Roots soak up water and other nutrients from the soil. These nutrients are carried to various parts of plants through the stem. Leaves are plant parts that trap light energy and make food for the plant.

Leaves are made of tissues and cells. A thin layer of rectangular cells covers all the surfaces of a leaf. This outer layer of cells is called the epidermis. The epidermis protects the inner parts of the leaf. The inside of a leaf is made of two layers of cells: the palisade cells and the spongy cells. The palisade cells are just below the epidermis. Under the palisade cells are the spongy cells. There is much air among the spongy cells.

Photosynthesis is the process by which the leaves of green plants use light energy to produce food. The word *photosynthesis* comes from the Greek words *photo,* meaning "light," and *synthesis,* meaning "putting together." Using light energy, green plants combine, or put together, water and carbon dioxide to make food and oxygen.

Recall that chlorophyll is a green substance present in most plants. Chlorophyll is contained in the **chloroplasts,** special structures found in palisade and spongy cells. The light energy needed for photosynthesis is absorbed by chlorophyll. The chlorophyll causes carbon dioxide and water to combine to produce oxygen and a simple sugar called glucose.

The oxygen produced during photosynthesis is given off into Earth's atmosphere through the leaves of a plant. How does oxygen exit the leaves of a plant? Gases such as oxygen, carbon dioxide, and water vapor exit and enter plant leaves through small openings in the leaves called **stomata.** Many leaves have nearly 15,000 stomata per square inch of

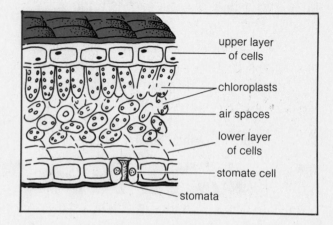

The illustration above shows the enlargement of a cross-section through a leaf of a green plant.

surface area. Most of these openings are found in the lower epidermis. During the day, the stomata are open. At night, the stomata are usually closed.

Many plants absorb more water from the air and ground than they are able to make use of. Much of the water that is not used during photosynthesis is lost through transpiration. **Transpiration** is the loss of water vapor through the stomata of a leaf. Some fruit trees lose about four gallons of water per hour on a hot, sunny day.

The glucose produced during photosynthesis may be used immediately by the plant, or it may be stored for use during periods when photosynthesis is difficult or impossible. Why do green plants make glucose? Green plants are able to combine glucose with other elements to produce the fats, proteins, and vitamins needed for the plant to survive. Green plants also get energy by breaking down the glucose made during photosynthesis. To get energy, plants combine the glucose with oxygen to produce carbon dioxide and water. This process of releasing energy from food is called **respiration.**

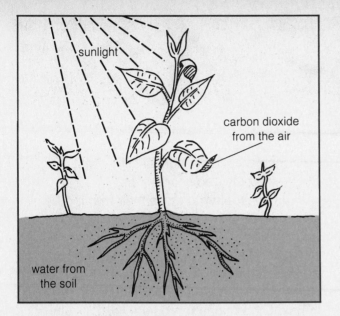

Plants can manufacture food from energy from the sun, carbon dioxide, and water.

Compare photosynthesis and respiration. During photosynthesis, energy is used by green plants to make glucose and oxygen. During respiration, glucose and oxygen are combined to release energy. Photosynthesis and respiration take place in all green plants. Animals and plants that are not green carry on respiration, but they do not carry on photosynthesis.

Plants are a very important part of food chains. Plants supply the oxygen needed for respiration. Some plants are eaten by people and other animals. The stored energy and nutrients in plants are thus passed on to the animals that eat them. Some plants are not eaten. Nutrients from these plants are returned to the soil by roots, or when the plants die. Life as we know it on this planet would not be possible without plants. ■

Lesson Review

Determine whether each of the following statements is true or false. Correct each false statement by crossing out the word or phrase that makes it false and by writing the correct word or phrase above it.

_____ 1. Roots trap light energy and make food for the plant.

_____ 2. The epidermis protects the inner parts of a leaf.

_____ 3. Transpiration is the process by which the leaves of green plants make food.

_____ 4. Chlorophyll is contained in chloroplasts.

_____ 5. During photosynthesis, carbon dioxide and water combine to form oxygen and glucose.

_____ 6. Gases enter and leave a leaf through the chloroplasts.

_____ 7. The loss of water vapor through the stomata is called respiration.

_____ 8. Glucose can be used immediately by a plant, or it can be stored for later use.

● _____ 9. Plants lose more moisture during the night.

● _____ 10. Cactus plants produce their own food.

Seedless Plants

Recall that botanists have identified over 275,000 species of plants. Think about all of the different kinds of plants in gardens, nurseries, forests, and oceans. How would you classify plants—by color, by size, by how they look?

Botanists have classified plants by their structures into two groups: nonvascular and vascular. **Nonvascular** plants are plants that have no connective tissues for carrying food and water throughout the plant. Because of this, nonvascular plants need to live in water to survive and reproduce. Algae, most mosses, and liverworts are nonvascular plants. **Vascular** plants are plants that have tissues for moving essential nutrients throughout the plant. Ferns, fruits, grasses, and trees are vascular plants.

Ferns are vascular plants with roots, leaves, and stems. Their leaves are called fronds.

Algae are simple nonvascular plants. Algae have no stems, roots, or leaves. All algae contain chlorophyll to make their own food. Most green algae grow in fresh water. Red algae and most brown algae live in salt water. Algae range in size from microscopic, one-celled organisms to plants over 200 feet in length! Some algae reproduce asexually by dividing in half. Other algae reproduce sexually when two cells, a sperm cell and an egg cell, unite to form a **zygote,** or fertilized egg cell. The zygote develops into a new plant.

Mosses are nonvascular plants that have no roots. They are attached to the ground by rootlike structures called rhizoids. Some mosses have stems. The leaves of most mosses are only one cell thick. Like algae, mosses produce their own food. Mosses live in moist places because, like algae, they need moisture to reproduce. Mosses are often found near the banks of streams and rivers, on wet walls, and under trees.

The life cycle of a moss is made up of a sexual phase and an asexual phase. During the sexual phase, a sperm cell joins with an egg cell to produce a zygote. The zygote grows into a new plant. At the top of the new plant is a cuplike structure that produces reproductive cells called **spores.** The production of spores starts the asexual phase of the life cycle of a moss. The spores fall to the ground and grow into new plants. With time, the new plants make sperm cells or egg cells, and the life cycle is repeated.

Simple vascular plants include ferns, horsetails, and club mosses. Unlike nonvascular plants, vascular plants live in land habitats because they do not depend on water to reproduce. Vascular plants also are much larger than nonvascular plants because they have tissues to transport water and nutrients throughout the plant. Ferns are vascular plants with roots, leaves, and stems. The feathery leaves of a fern are called fronds. The stems of most ferns grow undergound. So most ferns are only a few feet high. Some tropical ferns, however, grow as tall as 40 feet. Most ferns grow in wet, shady places.

The life cycle of a fern is asexual and sexual like that of a moss. In the asexual phase of a fern's life cycle, it makes spores. In the sexual phase, the fern makes sperm cells and egg cells. The fertilized eggs develop into large, spore-producing ferns, and the life cycle begins again.

Club mosses and horsetails are other simple vascular plants. Club mosses have roots, stems, and leaves. Like mosses, they grow in moist, wooded areas. The stem of a club moss grows along the ground. Roots extend from the stem onto the ground. A horsetail is a simple plant that has very small, scaly leaves that extend from its stem. Club mosses and horsetails produce spores that are enclosed in cones. ■

Lesson Review

On the line before each statement, write the letter of the choice that best completes the statement.

_____ 1. _____ plants have no connective tissues for transporting nutrients throughout the plant.

    a. Fern   b. Grass   c. Vascular   d. Nonvascular

_____ 2. _____ are nonvascular plants with no roots, stems, or leaves.

    a. Ferns   b. Trees   c. Mosses   d. Algae

_____ 3. A zygote is a fertilized _____ cell.

    a. sperm   b. egg   c. spore   d. plant

_____ 4. _____ are nonvascular plants without roots.

    a. Mosses   b. Fruits   c. Ferns   d. Trees

_____ 5. Mosses are attached to the ground by rootlike structures called _____.

    a. algae   b. stems   c. rhizoids   d. fronds

_____ 6. The production of _____ starts the asexual phase of reproduction in a moss.

    a. egg cells   b. sperm cells   c. spores   d. zygotes

_____ 7. _____ are vascular plants with roots, leaves and stems.

    a. Algae   b. Mosses   c. Ferns   d. All of the above

_____ 8. During the sexual phase of a fern's life cycle, _____ are produced.

    a. sperm cells and egg cells   b. spores   c. egg cells only   d. sperm cells only

• _____ 9. A maple tree is a(n) _____ plant.

    a. nonvascular   b. vascular   c. algae   d. moss

• _____ 10. _____ algae is commonly found in a freshwater aquarium containing goldfish.

    a. Red   b. Brown   c. Green   d. All of the above

Seed Plants

Seed plants include fruits, vegetables, flowers, shrubs, trees, and grasses. Seed plants are complex vascular plants that reproduce sexually from seeds. Inside each seed is a food supply that nourishes a young plant called an embryo. Around the seed is a protective cover called the seed coat. Botanists classify seed plants into two groups: gymnosperms and angiosperms.

Gymnosperms are seed plants whose seeds are not protected by being formed inside a fruit. Cicads, cypress, spruce, and redwoods are gymnosperms. Many gymnosperms, including pine trees and spruce trees, produce seeds that are in cones. These gymnosperms are called conifers, or cone-bearers. Conifers usually grow in cold, dry climates.

Conifers reproduce sexually when male cones produce pollen and release it into the air. The pollen is carried to female cones, which contain egg cells. A zygote forms and grows into a tiny embryo that eventually be-comes a seed. When the seed ripens, it falls to the ground where it may grow into a new plant.

Angiosperms are seed plants that produce seeds inside a fruit. Peaches, tomatoes, oaks, and nuts are only a few of the over 240,000 species of angiosperms. These plants have leaves and well-developed root systems. Angiosperms are often called flowering plants.

Flowers are made of both female and male structures. The male structures, or **stamens**, produce pollen grains. The female structures, or **pistils,** produce egg cells. The stamens and pistils are surrounded by petals. **Sepals** are tough, leaflike, green coverings that protect the young flower from cold and other injuries.

Flowering plants must be pollinated and fertilized to produce seeds. During **pollination,** wind, water, and animals carry pollen grains to the pistils of a flower. Self-pollination takes place when pollen is carried between the stamens and pistils on different flowers of the same plant. Cross-pollination is the transfer

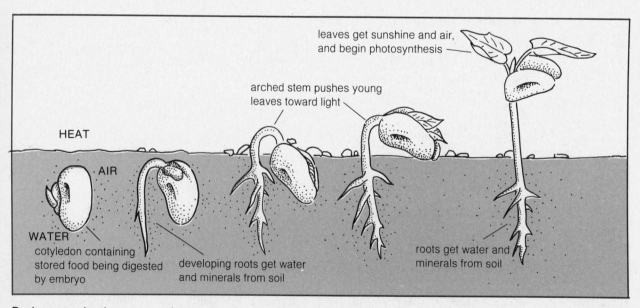

leaves get sunshine and air, and begin photosynthesis

arched stem pushes young leaves toward light

HEAT

AIR

WATER
cotyledon containing stored food being digested by embryo

developing roots get water and minerals from soil

roots get water and minerals from soil

During germination, many changes occur in a seed.

of pollen from the stamens of a flower on one plant to the pistils of a flower on another.

After the pollen grains are transferred to the pistils, a pollen tube grows down into the ovule of the flower. An **ovule** is the female part of the flower that contains the egg. When the pollen tube enters the ovule, fertilization occurs. **Fertilization** is the joining of the male and female sex cells to produce a zygote. The zygote grows into an embryo, and the ovule around it develops into a seed.

Different kinds of seeds need specific conditions to become plants. The kind of soil, its temperature, the amount of food stored in the seed, and the amount of moisture and air in the soil determine whether a seed will become a new plant. When the conditions are suitable, an embryo begins to grow into a young seedling. The early growth of a plant from a seed is called **germination.** During germination, the embryo pushes through its seed coat. Soon after, young leaves appear above the soil. These leaves contain stored

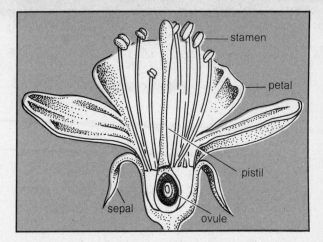

A flower is the reproductive organ in some seed plants.

food for the embryo. Roots develop, growing downward into the soil, and absorb water and other nutrients the plant needs. The nutrients are transported throughout the plant. When exposed to light energy, the leaves make food by photosynthesis. The young plant is now able to feed itself and provide oxygen to the many living things that depend on it. ■

Lesson Review

In the space before each number, write the letter of the word or group of words in Column 2 that matches the description in Column 1.

Column 1

_____ 1. contains a food supply for the embryo and is covered by the seed coat

_____ 2. plants whose seeds are not protected by a fruit

_____ 3. gymnosperms that produce seeds in cones

_____ 4. produce pollen in conifers

_____ 5. seed plants that produce seeds inside a fruit

_____ 6. leaflike coverings that protect young flowers

_____ 7. transfer of pollen

_____ 8. the early growth of a plant from a seed

● _____ 9. an example of an angiosperm

● _____ 10. an example of a gymnosperm

Column 2

a. angiosperms

b. a redwood tree

c. germination

d. gymnosperms

e. male cones

f. pine trees

g. pollination

h. seed

i. sepals

j. a walnut tree

Plant Genetics

If you plant corn seeds, you expect to grow corn. If you plant seeds from red poppies, you expect red poppies to bloom. Young plants and animals tend to very closely resemble their parents. The passing of certain traits from parents to their offspring is known as **heredity.** The scientific study of heredity is **genetics.**

In the mid-1800s, Gregor Mendel, an Austrian monk, was one of the first people to study heredity in plants. He conducted experiments to study the inheritance of seven pairs of traits in pea plants. The traits he studied were short or tall stems, smooth or wrinkled seeds, even or clustered distribution of flowers along the stalk, green or yellow pods, red or white flowers, full or shrunken pods, and yellow or green seeds.

Mendel grew the plants he studied from self-pollinated pea plants. The self-pollinated plants produced the same plants in successive generations. For example, one type of plant had green seeds. Another had yellow seeds. Mendel cross-pollinated these plants with both colors of seeds. All the new plants in the first generation had yellow seeds. Mendel concluded from these results that yellow was a dominant trait of seed color, while green was the recessive trait of seed color. A **dominant trait** is one that shows up and prevents another trait from being seen. A **recessive trait** is one that is masked or hidden when the dominant trait appears. The other recessive traits Mendel observed in his study of pea plants were short stems, wrinkled seeds, white flowers, flowers clustered at one end of the stalk, yellow pods, and shrunken pods.

Recall that all living things are made of cells, the building blocks of life. Most cells contain a **nucleus,** which holds the genetic material deoxyribonucleic acid, or DNA. The DNA forms a code, which is carried on threadlike structures called **chromosomes.** Chromosomes are made of genes. **Genes** control the inheritance of traits from parents to the offspring of the parents.

A **hybrid form** of a trait results when dominant and recessive genes combine. Mendel had found that the first generation of cross-pollinated plants showed only the dominant trait. The second generation of these pea plants, however, showed the dominant trait three times as often as it showed the recessive trait.

What Mendel had discovered about inheritance in pea plants is important to geneticists, scientists who study genetics. It has been discovered, however, that many traits show a wide variation and are not necessarily inherited in the three-to-one ratios discovered by Mendel.

Have you ever eaten a watermelon without seeds? Does your grass stay green in very hot, dry weather? Can plants be bred to withstand extreme weather conditions such as drought or cold? Is it possible to develop plants that are resistant to diseases? Can bigger and better fruits and vegetables be "made to order"? The answers to these questions are provided by the science of genetic engineering. Genetic engineering is also looking for answers to other questions.

Scientists who work in the field of genetic engineering have made important advances in many areas. Researchers are now able, for example, to study genes from the cells of unborn babies. They can tell whether or not the babies will be born with certain diseases. They hope someday to be able to treat babies for certain diseases before they are born. Using the techniques of genetic

Through the use of plant genetics, scientists may one day develop peaches without pits.

engineering, scientists are also working in other areas that might produce useful results. For example, they are currently working on the development of organisms that will break down solid wastes into easily disposed substances.

Genetic engineering involves the moving of genes from one organism to the genetic material of another organism. The new organism has traits of both organisms. Similarly, through **cloning**, new plants can be developed from one cell of a certain plant. Cloning produces offspring that have traits that are identical to those of the parent cell. Genetic engineering also can be used to produce offspring with traits different from those traits of the parents. So the next time you bite into a juicy ripe tomato, keep in mind that it may be a product of genetic engineering. ■

Lesson Review

In the space provided, write the word or words that best complete the statement.

1. The passing of traits from parents to offspring is _____.

2. _____ studied the inheritance of traits in pea plants in the mid-1800s.

3. The first generation of plants used by Mendel were _____-pollinated.

4. A _____ trait is one that masks another form of the trait.

5. The _____ of a cell contains the genetic material, DNA.

6. _____ control the inheritance of traits from parents to offspring.

7. A _____ form of a trait is the result of the combination of dominant and recessive genes.

8. _____ involves the moving of genes from one organism to the genetic material of another organism.

● 9. When peas that bear white flowers are crossed with peas that bear red flowers, all the flowers of the first generation of offspring will be _____ in color.

● 10. When peas with tall stems are bred with peas with short stems, the first generation will have the _____ trait of height.

55

Horticulturists specialize in the raising of vegetables, fruits, flowers, and ornamental trees and shrubs.

Botanists are biologists who specialize in the study of plants and the environment in which the plants grow. Some botanists study all aspects of plant life, while others specialize in specific areas such as the identification and classification of plants. Some botanists focus their research on the diseases of plants and the search for cures. Many botanists are involved with research at the university level. Some botanists work for companies in the food industry. Companies that produce fertilizers and insecticides also employ botanists. Government agencies, both federal and state, which are involved in agriculture and conservation, have botanists on their staffs.

Horticulturists specialize in the raising of vegetables, fruits, flowers, and ornamental trees and shrubs. Some work for private companies in the food business. Others work for companies that supply plants to florists and nurseries. Some horticulturists are employed by the government at agricultural experiment stations. Still others work for nonprofit foundations that manage arboretums and botanical gardens.

Agronomists are scientists who study crops and the soils in which they grow. Many agronomists search for methods that will increase the production of food crops. These agronomists determine how to make soil more productive. They investigate the effectiveness of various fertilizers and conduct experiments in crop rotation, irrigation, and drainage. Many agronomists are employed by companies that grow and distribute fruit and vegetables. Some agronomists work for federal and state agricultural agencies that provide assistance and advice to farmers.

Ecologists study the relationships that living things have to one another and to their surroundings. Some ecologists are concerned with the supply of food that is available to feed an ever-increasing human population. Other ecologists try to identify environmental problems that might develop if changes occur in a particular land area. Private research institutions and consulting firms employ ecologists, and many ecologists work for federal agencies, such as the Soil Conservation Service, the Forest Service, and the Bureau of Land Management.

Job opportunities for those who have an interest in plants are available with many agricultural and conservation organizations. These facilities employ people to work in crop production and forestry management. Nurseries and landscaping companies have a need for people who are interested in caring for plants and in using plants for decorative purposes. Government agencies and private foundations often seek workers who can assist with agricultural improvement and land conservation programs. ■

For Further Information

More information about these and related careers is available from the following publications and organizations.

Working for Life: Careers in Biology, Thomas H. Easton, Plexus, 1988

Careers in Horticultural Sciences, Dorothy Dowdell, Messner, 1975

Opportunities in Biological Sciences, Charles A. Winter, National Textbook Company, 1984

American Institute of Biological Sciences
1401 Wilson Boulevard
Arlington, VA 22209

American Society of Horticultural Science
701 North Saint Asaph Street
Alexandria, VA 22314

Animals

Horses are vertebrates that reproduce by internal fertilization.

Lesson 1

Characteristics of Animals

Recall that biologists have classified living things into five kingdoms based on their likenesses and differences. The two kingdoms that you probably know the most about are the plant kingdom and the animal kingdom. Recall that most plants cannot move about and that they make their own food. Most animals can move about. Animals swim, walk, run, crawl, slither, or fly. However, animals rely on plants or other animals for food.

Scientists have identified over two million species of animals but believe that about four million species exist. The branch of biology that studies animals is **zoology.** Zoologists, scientists who study animals, have classified animals into nine main phyla and several smaller phyla. Phyla are subdivisions of a kingdom, such as the animal kingdom.

Of the twelve or so phyla in the animal kingdom, all vertebrates belong to one phylum. A **vertebrate** is an animal with a backbone.

The backbone helps to protect the spinal cord, or main nerve cord, of a vertebrate. Vertebrates have an internal skeleton that is connected to the backbone. The skeleton provides support for the animal and protects its internal organs. People, snakes, fish, birds, frogs, dogs, cats, sheep, and turtles are only a few of the many vertebrates in the animal kingdom.

About 95 percent of all known animal species are invertebrates. An **invertebrate** is an animal without a backbone. Invertebrates do not have internal skeletons. Insects, worms, lobsters, and sponges are invertebrates.

Some animals reproduce asexually. Asexual reproduction involves only one parent. **Budding** is a form of asexual reproduction in which a small bud develops on the surface of the parent, grows, separates, and forms a new organism. **Regeneration** is a form of asexual reproduction in which lost body parts are regrown, or regenerated.

Sexual reproduction in animals involves two parents. Males produce sperm and females produce eggs. Sperm fertilize the eggs to form zygotes. The zygotes develop into new animals.

In vertebrates, sexual reproduction can result from external fertilization or internal fertilization. **External fertilization** is the joining of the sperm and egg outside the female's body. Fish and frogs reproduce by external fertilization. **Internal fertilization** occurs when the egg is fertilized inside the female body. Many vertebrates, including birds, and mammals, reproduce by internal fertilization.

Animals are complex organisms. They are born with some behaviors. They learn other behaviors. **Inborn behavior** is behavior that is inherited from the parents. A bird flying, a fish swimming, and a person pulling her hand away from fire are examples of inborn behaviors. **Acquired behavior** is behavior that is learned. Training a pet to do a trick or learning to read are examples of acquired behavior.

How does an animal survive in its habitat? What happens if the habitat changes?

Recall that a habitat is the place in which an organism naturally lives. When an animal's environment changes for long periods of time, the animal must adapt to survive. An **adaptation** is a trait that helps an organism to survive in its environment. Many desert plants have waxy coverings that prevent water loss. Fish have gills that allow them to take in oxygen from the water in which they live. A woodpecker uses its sharp beak to hammer at a tree in order to find food. Penguins have layers of fat and feathers that keep them warm during the polar winters. Waxy coverings, gills, beaks, and layers of fat and feathers are adaptations.

What happens when animals are not able to adapt to their environments? Consider what happened to dinosaurs. Dinosaurs were animals that inhabited Earth millions of years ago. Most scientists believe that a large meteorite struck Earth and caused global climatic changes. Dinosaurs and many other organisms were not able to adapt to the new environment. This led to the **extinction,** or the total disappearance, of many species. ∎

Lesson Review

In the space provided, write the word or words that best complete the statement.

1. The branch of biology that focuses mainly on the study of animals is _____.

2. A(n) _____ is an animal with a backbone.

3. Vertebrates have _____ that protect internal organs and provide support.

4. A(n) _____ is an animal without a backbone.

5. Budding is a form of _____ reproduction in animals.

6. Fish and frogs reproduce by _____ fertilization.

7. _____ fertilization occurs when the egg is fertilized inside the body of the female.

8. _____ behavior is behavior that is learned.

● 9. Dinosaurs became extinct because they could not _____ to their new environment.

● 10. Blinking the eyes is a(n) _____ behavior.

Mammals

What do you have in common with kangaroos, armadillos, giraffes, pigs, cows, bats, and whales? All of these animals are mammals. **Mammals** are vertebrates that have hair on their bodies and produce milk to feed their young. Mammals range in size from bats that are about the size of bees to blue whales, which fully grown can exceed 100 feet in length.

Most mammals live on land. Most of these land mammals move about on either four legs or two legs and walk by lifting one foot at a time. Humans, giraffes, horses, bears, and pigs are terrestrial, or land, mammals. Some mammals spend much of their lives in trees. These arboreal, or tree, mammals have adaptations that allow them to climb trees and to move from tree to tree. Squirrels, sloths, and chipmunks are arboreal mammals. Aquatic mammals are mammals that live in water. Whales, porpoises, and dolphins are aquatic mammals. Bats are the only mammals that can fly.

Mammals are warm-blooded animals. A **warm-blooded animal** has an almost constant body temperature. Warm-blooded animals must be protected from extreme cold and heat. The hair or fur on mammals often helps to provide protection. Fur or hair also protects a mammal from its enemies. The fur may be a color that blends in with the animal's surroundings, camouflaging the animal from its predators.

Because most warm-blooded vertebrates are very active, their hearts must be adapted to the greater need for oxygen. A mammal has a four-chambered heart. Two chambers pump blood to the lungs and back to the heart again. The other two chambers pump blood that is returning from the lungs to the rest of the animal's body.

Nearly all mammals have teeth with which they catch or chew food. Most mammals are herbivores. **Herbivores** are animals that eat plants. The teeth of herbivores are broad and flat and are used for grinding food. **Carnivores** are animals that eat other animals. Most carnivores have long, pointed teeth that they use to tear food. Some mammals eat both plants and animals and are called **omnivores.** Omnivores have pointed teeth to tear food and broad, flat teeth to grind or chew food. Bats are insectivores, or insect-eating animals.

The digestive systems of mammals differ depending on the kind of food they eat. Carnivores have simple stomachs and short

Dolphins are aquatic animals. Mammals are warm-blooded animals that usually care for their young until they are fully developed.

intestines. Herbivores have complex stomachs and long intestines. Cows are mammals that eat grass. What kinds of teeth and digestive systems do they have?

Mammals reproduce by the internal fertilization of a female egg by a male sperm. The zygote that forms grows into an embryo that develops into a new animal. The offspring of most mammals develop completely inside the female's body before birth.

Two groups of mammals, however, are exceptions to this trait of mammals. Marsupials, such as kangaroos, koala bears, and opossums, are born not fully developed. After birth, the young mammal crawls into the mother's pouch and attaches itself to one of the mother's mammary glands. Then, after birth, the young mammal is fed at the mother's mammary gland. The mammary glands produce milk and provide nourishment for the developing animal. Some mammals, including the duckbilled platypus, lay eggs protected by leathery shells. The female keeps the eggs warm until they hatch. The hatchlings feed on milk from the mother until they are fully developed.

Mammals produce fewer offspring than most other animals. How then can a species of mammals survive if so few offspring are produced? Mammals are unique among animals because most mammals care for their young after birth. Care of the offspring helps to ensure the survival of the species. ∎

Lesson Review

In the space before each number, write the letter of the word or group of words in Column 2 that matches the description in Column 1.

Column 1

_____ 1. vertebrates with hair or fur that care for their young after birth

_____ 2. mammals that live in water

_____ 3. this organ pumps blood through the body of a mammal

_____ 4. animals that eat plants

_____ 5. bats are these types of eaters

_____ 6. are not fully developed at birth and continue development in a pouch

_____ 7. produce milk in mammals

_____ 8. lays eggs protected by leathery shells

● _____ 9. based on what they eat, most humans are these

● _____ 10. habitats of monkeys make them this kind of mammal

Column 2

a. aquatic mammals

b. arboreal mammals

c. four-chambered heart

d. herbivores

e. insectivores

f. mammals

g. mammary glands

h. marsupials

i. omnivores

j. duckbilled platypus

Birds and Insects

Birds are warm-blooded vertebrates whose bodies are covered with feathers. The feathers provide protection from heat and cold. Feathers also aid in flight. A bird's wings are curved on top and basically flat or just slightly curved on the bottom. As a bird moves forward, air flows more rapidly over the wing than under it. This lowers the air pressure above the wing. The higher pressure below the wing pushes the wing upward, allowing the bird to overcome gravity and fly. Although all birds have wings, not all birds can fly.

Birds reproduce sexually. Fertilization of the egg takes place inside the female's body. Then the female lays the eggs.

Most birds eat worms, fruits, seeds, and insects. Eagles, hawks, and owls eat small animals such as mice and rabbits. Some water birds eat fish. But unlike most other vertebrates, birds have no teeth. Their **beaks,** or bills, are hard, bony mouthparts that are adapted to the kinds of food birds eat. A woodpecker has a sharp beak for drilling into wood to gather insects. Meat-eating birds have sharp, curved beaks for tearing at food.

A bird has two legs with feet that are adapted for the way in which the bird moves.

Birds that spend a great deal of time flying have short legs. Wading birds have long legs. Among many birds, three toes point forward and one toe points backward. Some birds have toes that are adapted for climbing; two toes point forward and two point backward. Birds that swim have webs of skin that connect the toes, allowing these birds to use their feet as paddles. Birds of prey, such as eagles and hawks, have sharp claws, or talons, which allow them to hold the small animals they eat.

Most species of birds eat insects. **Insects** are small, complex invertebrates with jointed legs, segmented bodies, and a hard, external skeleton called an **exoskeleton.** When most people think of insects, they think of those insects that damage crops and plants, those that are pests, and those that spread diseases. However, of the over 800,000 known species of insects, less than one percent is harmful.

The body of most insects has three distinct parts: the head, the thorax, and the abdomen. The head of an insect includes its brain, mouth, eyes, and other sensory organs. **Antennae,** the long, slender feelers on an insect's head, are located between the eyes. Depending upon the type of insect, the

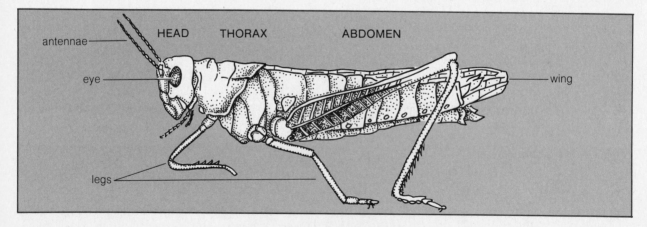

Many insects have external features similar to those of a grasshopper

antennae are used to feel, smell, taste, and hear. Behind the head is the **thorax,** or upper body, to which the legs and wings of an insect are attached. Most insects have six legs that are used to walk, hop, or swim. Insects make sounds by rubbing their legs or wings together. Most insects have at least one pair of wings. Some insects have two pairs of wings. Fleas are insects that have no wings. The insect's **abdomen** is behind the thorax and is used to digest food, remove wastes, reproduce, and breathe.

Nearly all insects lay eggs. After hatching from the eggs, most insects begin the larva

stage. The larva eats a great deal and grows very quickly. The larva spins a cocoon or other protective covering to prepare for the next life stage. The larva of a butterfly is a caterpillar. The larva of a fly is a maggot.

When the larva is fully grown, it enters the pupa stage. From the outside, the pupa appears to be inactive. However, inside the protective covering, the pupa is developing into an adult insect. When the insect is fully developed, it breaks through the cocoon or protective covering and emerges as an adult insect. This series of changes, or growth stages, is called **metamorphosis.** ∎

Lesson Review

Fill in the circle containing the letter of the term or phrase that correctly completes each statement.

1. A bird's _____ provide protection from heat and cold, and aid in flight.
   - (a) wings
   - (b) beaks
   - (c) webbed feet
   - (d) feathers

2. Birds eat _____.
   - (a) worms
   - (b) small animals
   - (c) insects
   - (d) all of the above

3. A bird's _____ are adapted to the kinds of food birds eat.
   - (a) teeth
   - (b) feet and legs
   - (c) talons
   - (d) beaks

4. Wading birds usually have _____.
   - (a) long legs
   - (b) talons
   - (c) sharp beaks
   - (d) none of the above

5. Insects are complex invertebrates with _____.
   - (a) an exoskeleton
   - (b) jointed legs
   - (c) segmented bodies
   - (d) all of the above

6. The antennae of an insect are located on the _____.
   - (a) head
   - (b) abdomen
   - (c) thorax
   - (d) legs

7. Insects make sounds with their _____.
   - (a) mouths
   - (b) legs and wings
   - (c) ears
   - (d) abdomens

8. The _____ spins the protective covering in the life cycle of an insect.
   - (a) egg
   - (b) larva
   - (c) pupa
   - (d) adult

● 9. A pelican is a water bird with a flat, broad beak. The diet of a pelican is mainly _____.
   - (a) insects
   - (b) fruit
   - (c) fish
   - (d) seeds

● 10. A difference in _____ allows birds to fly.
   - (a) claws
   - (b) air pressure
   - (c) wing structure
   - (d) tail feathers

Amphibians and Reptiles

Frogs, toads, and salamanders are among the 3,000 known species of amphibians. **Amphibians** are cold-blooded vertebrates that live part of their lives in water and part of their lives on land. A **cold-blooded animal** is one that cannot keep a constant body temperature. Its body temperature rises and falls as the temperature of its environment changes.

With a few exceptions, amphibians have smooth, moist skin. The skin of some toads, however, is rough and leathery. The skin and lungs of amphibians take in oxygen and release carbon dioxide. While in water, an adult amphibian breathes through its skin. On land, it breathes with its lungs. In some species of frogs and salamanders, the color of the skin changes to match its environment and acts as camouflage to protect the animal.

Amphibians reproduce sexually. The eggs of most amphibians are laid and fertilized in water. The eggs of some salamanders, however, are fertilized inside the female amphibian before they are laid.

Like insects, amphibians undergo metamorphosis. The first stage of metamorphosis in an amphibian is a tadpole. Tadpoles breathe through **gills,** which are small slits located behind the head. Tadpoles have long tails for swimming. Several days after hatching from the egg, a tadpole develops hind legs. As a tadpole ages, its front legs develop and the shape of its head changes. Soon, tadpoles lose their gills and develop lungs. The tail is eventually absorbed into the body. Metamorphosis in some amphibians, such as frogs, takes several weeks. Other species take years to develop.

Snakes, crocodiles, alligators, lizards, and turtles are reptiles. **Reptiles** are cold-blooded vertebrates with dry, scaly skins that keep in water. Reptiles live mainly on land. What kind of breathing organs do they have?

Scientists have classified reptiles according to their body structures. The three main groups are lizards and snakes, turtles, and crocodiles and alligators. Lizards and snakes have hard scales covering their bodies. Most species of lizards have four legs and live in warm habitats. Lizards hear through ear openings and see with eyes that may have eyelids. Snakes have no legs; hear through bones in their skulls; and have eyes with no eyelids. Snakes shed their skin several times a year in a process called **molting.**

Turtles are reptiles with bony shells that protect and support their bodies. Turtles are able to live on land, in fresh water, and in

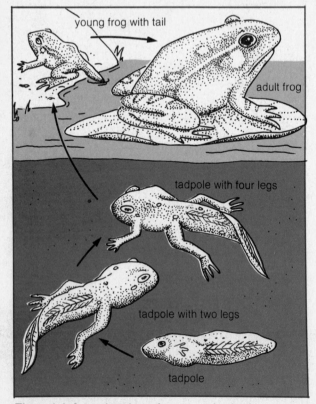

young frog with tail

adult frog

tadpole with four legs

tadpole with two legs

tadpole

The adult frog develops from a tadpole.

salt water. Land turtles, or tortoises, have claws on their feet that are adapted for walking and digging. Water turtles have either webbed feet or flippers used for swimming. Most turtles have sharp beaks to tear their food.

There are about 20 species of crocodiles and alligators. These reptiles live in or near water. Crocodiles and alligators look similar in shape and size. Both have very strong jaws and powerful tails. Both breathe through nostrils in their snouts.

Reptiles reproduce by internal fertilization. Most reptiles lay their eggs on land. The eggs have tough, leathery shells that keep them from drying out. The young hatch from the eggs. Only a few species of reptiles care directly for their young.

Most reptiles are carnivores, or meat eaters. Snakes are carnivores. Poisonous snakes have hollow teeth, or fangs, that inject venom into their prey. **Prey** is an animal that is eaten by another animal. Nonpoisonous snakes usually swallow their prey alive. Snakes do not chew their food. Their teeth move the prey into the throat where it is swallowed whole. ■

The tree toad is a land-dwelling amphibian.

Lesson Review

In the space provided, write the word or words that best complete the statement.

1. _____ are cold-blooded vertebrates that live part of their lives on land and part in water.

2. A(n) _____ animal is one that cannot keep a constant body temperature.

3. Amphibians take in oxygen through their _____ and lungs.

4. The first stage of metamorphosis in an amphibian is a(n) _____.

5. _____ are cold-blooded vertebrates with dry, scaly skins that keep in water.

6. Lizards hear through _____ openings.

7. Snakes shed their skin several times a year in a process called _____.

8. _____ turtles have webbed feet or flippers.

● 9. A live mouse might become _____ for a nonpoisonous snake.

● 10. From the time they hatch, _____ breathe through lungs.

Fish

Many people believe that most water animals are fish. Of starfish, dolphins, turtles, oysters, and tuna, only tuna are fish. Starfish and oysters are invertebrates. Dolphins are mammals. What are turtles?

Fish are cold-blooded vertebrates that live in fresh water or salt water and get oxygen from the water through gills. Ichthyologists, scientists who study fish, have identified over 21,000 species of fish. Fish can be divided into three groups: jawless fish, bony fish, and cartilage fish. Jawless fish, such as the lamprey, have suckerlike mouths lined with teeth. Their skeletons are made of **cartilage,** a tough, flexible tissue. Bony fish have hinged jaws, skeletons made of bone, and fins. **Fins** are bony structures covered with webs of skin and are moved by muscles. Tuna, trout, perch, bluegills, and eels are only a few of the thousands of species of bony fish. Cartilage fish, such as sharks, have hinged jaws that can open and close. Their skeletons are made of cartilage. Most cartilage fish have paired fins that aid swimming.

Fish get oxygen from the water through their gills. Recall that gills are small slits located behind the heads of certain vertebrates. Most fish have four gills on each side of the body. As water passes over the gills, oxygen is pulled into the blood. At the same time, carbon dioxide, a waste product, goes from the fish's blood into the water as it passes over the gills.

A fish has a two-chambered heart that pumps blood through its body. Because fish are cold-blooded animals, their body temperatures change with the water temperature. Some fish have a body temperature close to the freezing point of water. Other fish are as warm as 100°F.

Most fish have streamlined bodies to move through the water efficiently and effectively. The swimming movement of fish is caused by the contraction of muscles along their bodies. This causes a series of waves to pass down the length of the fish's body. Fish are thrust forward by the back-and-forth movement of their bodies. The tail controls direction.

A shark is a cartilage fish.

Fins, too, aid most fish in swimming by pushing back water. Most fish swim at rates of less than five miles per hour. Barracuda, however, can exceed speeds of 27 miles per hour!

Most fish are carnivores. Recall that a carnivore is an animal that eats meat. Carnivorous fish eat worms, shellfish, small fish, and zooplankton. **Zooplankton** are small, drifting or weakly swimming animals near the surface of many bodies of water. Most zooplankton can be seen only with the aid of a microscope. The largest fish, a species of shark that weighs about twice as much as an elephant, survives mainly on zooplankton.

Fish feed by two methods. Filter feeding is a method of feeding by which fish passively capture their prey as water passes through their mouths and over the gills. Salmon and some species of sharks are filter feeders. Other fish get food by using their senses to actively find and capture their prey.

Most fish reproduce by external fertilization. Female fish lay eggs in the water that are fertilized by male fish. Many bony fish that live in the oceans lay over a million eggs at one time. Certain fish reproduce by internal fertilization. The young of certain species of sharks completely develop in the oviduct of the female shark. ■

Lesson Review

In the space provided, write the word or words that best complete the statement.

1. Fish can be divided into three groups: _____,
   _____, and _____ fish.

2. _____ fish have suckerlike mouths lined with teeth.

3. Bony structures covered with webs of skin that aid fish in swimming
   are _____.

4. Fish obtain oxygen from the water through their _____.

5. A fish has a _____ heart that pumps blood through its body.

6. The basic swimming movement of fish is caused by the _____ of
   muscles along their bodies.

7. _____ are small, drifting or weakly swimming animals near the surface of a body of water.

8. _____ is a method of feeding in which food is passively cap-
   tured as water passes through the mouth and over the gills of a fish.

● 9. As the water temperature gets colder, a fish's body temperature
   gets _____.

● 10. Rays and skates have flattened bodies and jaws that can open and close. Their skeletons
   are made of cartilage. Rays and skates are classified as _____ fish.

Protecting Animals

The American bison, or buffalo, is a large animal. The length of an adult male ranges from ten to 12 feet. A fully grown male can be five to six feet tall and weigh as much as 3,000 pounds. Such an animal would never appear to be in much danger. Yet, the American bison nearly became extinct. Recall that extinction is the total disappearance of a species.

During the middle of the nineteenth century, about 60 million American bisons thundered in large herds across the plains of the American west. However, as the population of the United States moved westward, hunters slaughtered millions of these animals. By 1890, only about 50 bison survived in the United States. Only then did people begin to realize the need to preserve the bison. **Wildlife preservation** is the maintaining of a species to protect it from becoming extinct. Due to wildlife preservation efforts, more than 15,000 American bisons survive today in protected areas.

Extinction can be a natural process. Some species of animals become extinct due to natural changes in their environments. For example, most scientists believe that hundreds of millions of years ago dinosaurs became extinct because of severe climatic changes on our planet. Other prehistoric animals became extinct because the number of predators that hunted these animals increased. Still other animals vanished because of changes in the food supply. Most animals at risk today, however, are threatened because of human activities.

Illegal hunting practices have reduced wildlife populations. The African elephant, for example, is hunted for its ivory tusks. **Poaching,** or illegal hunting, of these animals has greatly reduced their numbers. To aid in the preservation of the African elephant, importing ivory is now illegal in many countries.

In what other ways do human activities threaten wildlife? Clearing forests, plowing grasslands, and draining and damming bodies of water affect many wildlife habitats. The invasion of wildlife habitats by people reduces the space available for animals to roam, gather food, and reproduce. Human development of land has greatly contributed to the near extinction of the Bengal tiger of India.

Many wildlife populations also have been harmed by poisonous chemicals that are used to control weeds, insects, and other pests. One such chemical, DDT, builds up in the fat cells of animals. Animals that eat contaminated animals pass the harmful substance through food chains. DDT is largely responsible for the plight of the bald eagle. The bald eagle feeds mainly on fish. Fish can often have concentrates of DDT in their bodies. The DDT builds up in the bald eagle's body and then, because of DDT, their eggs have very thin shells. The shells are so thin that the eggs are often crushed before they hatch. Even if the eggs are not crushed, the DDT can kill the chick before it hatches.

Biologists who study threatened animals classify them into three categories: rare species, threatened species, and endangered species. A **rare species** is a species that has very few living members. Rare species live in protected areas and therefore their numbers are not decreasing. A **threatened species** is one that is common in some areas, but their populations are generally decreasing in number. The gray wolf, for example, is very plentiful in some areas, yet it has been hunted, trapped, and poisoned to such an extent that it has vanished from some locations where it once roamed. An **endangered species** is a species that must be protected so that it does not become extinct. The California condor, the largest flying bird in the United States, is an endangered species. Only about a dozen or so condors still exist.

In the past 50 years, scientists have estimated that about one vertebrate species per year became extinct. How can rare, threatened, and endangered species be kept from becoming extinct? Many countries have set up wildlife refuges where hunting is against the law and the land is not available for development. In the United States, nearly 300 protected areas are part of the National Park System. More than 400 other areas are managed by the National Wildlife Refuge System.

The need to protect animal wildlife is vital to humans. In addition to their beauty and scientific value, every species of animal plays an important role in helping to maintain

The American bison was threatened with extinction in the early nineteenth century.

Earth's delicate biological balance. The extinction of any species can threaten the extinction of all species, including human beings. ■

Lesson Review

Identify each of the following statements as true or false. Correct each false statement by crossing out the word or phrase that makes it false and by writing the correct word or phrase above it.

_____ 1. The American bison was reduced in number because there was too much food.

_____ 2. Some extinctions are due to natural causes.

_____ 3. The California condor is an extinct species.

_____ 4. A rare species has few members, but their populations are not decreasing.

_____ 5. Wildlife preservation is the maintaining of a species to protect it from becoming extinct.

_____ 6. Poaching of certain animals has greatly increased their numbers.

_____ 7. Overhunting has contributed in part to making gray wolves a threatened species.

_____ 8. National Parks play no role in the protection of certain animal species.

● _____ 9. The clearing of a forest provides more food for herbivores.

● _____ 10. Large animals do not become in danger of extinction.

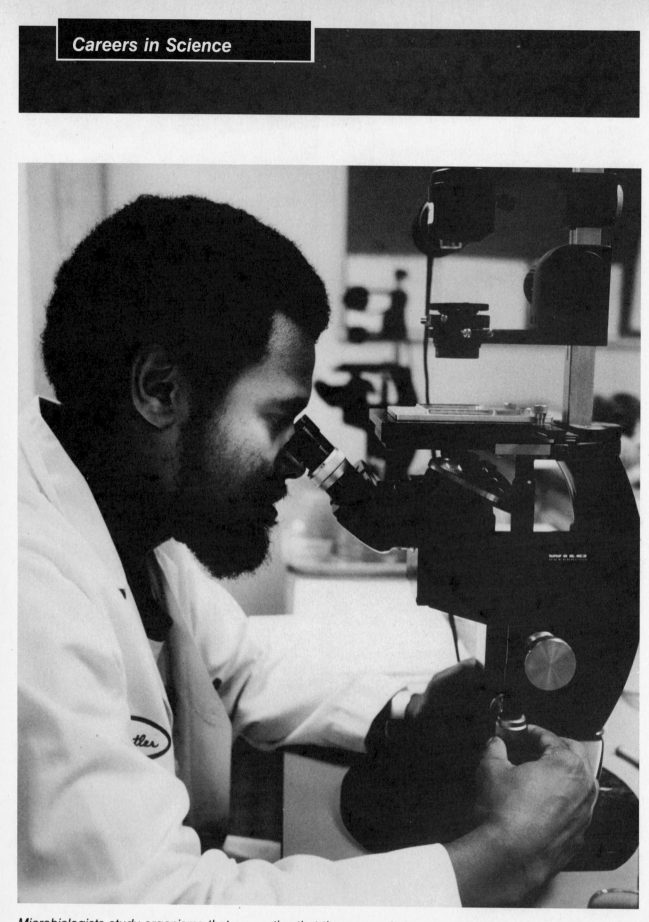

Microbiologists study organisms that are so tiny that they can only be seen through a microscope.

Zoologists are biologists who study animal life. Since the animal kingdom is so vast, a typical zoologist will focus on only a small part of it. Some zoologists study groups of animals, such as insects or birds. Others specialize in the causes of animal diseases and what can be done to prevent them. Some zoologists concentrate on animal development. Still others are concerned with the distribution of animals in the various parts of the world. Many zoologists teach and conduct research in colleges and universities. Some are employed by companies that produce food and drugs for animals. Some zoologists are associated with wildlife reserves and zoological gardens, or zoos. Some prepare exhibits and preserve specimens in museums. Zoologists also work for the federal and state governments.

Veterinarians specialize in the treatment of animals for diseases and injuries. Veterinarians who are in private practice in cities deal almost exclusively with house pets. Veterinarians who practice in rural areas spend most of their time keeping livestock healthy. Some veterinarians are associated with zoos. Certain veterinarians are associated with government agencies and specialize in the study and treatment of wildlife. Other veterinarians devote themselves exclusively to research at a university or at an institution operated by a federal or state agency.

Marine biologists study the organisms that live in the ocean. Some of these scientists study whales. Others focus on tiny organisms that can only be seen under a microscope. Many marine biologists work in specially equipped laboratories that are associated with universities or with private institutions. Companies in the seafood industry also employ marine biologists. Other marine biologists work for drug companies that obtain substances from the sea that are used in certain kinds of drugs.

Microbiologists are scientists who study organisms that are so tiny they can only be viewed through a microscope. Microbiologists study bacteria, protozoa, viruses, or fungi. Many microbiologists work for institutions, such as a Center for Disease Control. Some microbiologists are associated with universities where they teach and do research on micro-organisms. Others staff medical centers where they test samples sent in by private physicians. Microbiologists may also work for companies in the drug, chemical, and food processing industries.

In the field of animal science, a variety of positions is available for those who like to work closely with animals. Zoos are found in virtually all large cities and employ many people who care directly for the animals in their collections. Veterinarians employ trained assistants to help them provide services to animals. Many biological laboratories hire and train assistants and technicians to work with samples and specimens that are tested and analyzed. ■

For Further Information

More information about these and related careers is available from the following publications and organizations.

Careers in the Life Sciences, National Association of Biology Teachers, 1979

Careers Working with Animals, Humane Society of the United States, Acropolis Books, 1979

Career Guide to the Animal Health Field, M. L. Simmons, Wiley, 1983

Careers in the Animal Kingdom, Walter Oleksy, Simon & Schuster, 1980

American Society of Zoologists
California Lutheran College
Thousand Oaks, CA 91360

American Veterinary Medical Association
930 North Meacham Road
Schaumburg, IL 60172

American Society of Microbiology
1913 Eye Street, NW
Washington, DC 20006

The Human Body

Human beings are made of hundreds of trillions of cells.

Lesson 1

Body Basics

Anatomy is the study of the structure of the body. Physiology is the study of the jobs that are done by various parts of the body. Through the study of human anatomy and physiology, medical personnel have found ways to treat people who are sick or injured.

Recall that all organisms are made of cells, the building blocks of life. Humans are made of hundreds of trillions of cells. Cells in the human body are microscopic, which means they can be seen only with the aid of a microscope. Cells change food into energy; dispose of wastes; respond to stimuli; and reproduce.

There are many kinds of cells in the human body. Each type of cell performs a certain function. Nerve cells carry messages throughout the body. Blood cells transport food, oxygen, and carbon dioxide to and from the heart. Muscle cells contract and relax. Skin cells protect the body from disease.

Although all cells are unique, they are alike in some ways. Most cells have a ball-shaped nucleus that controls the activities of the cell. The nucleus is usually found near the center of the cell. The nucleus of the cell contains the chromosomes the cell needs to reproduce. All cells have a cell membrane, a thin layer of proteins and fats that holds the parts of the cell together. The cell membrane surrounds the cell and controls the movement of substances into and out of the cell. Within this membrane, all cells contain cytoplasm. Cytoplasm is a jellylike substance that contains the cell's proteins, waste products, and nutrients.

The cytoplasm houses many cell structures. Small, tubelike structures in the cytoplasm form a transportation network called the **endoplasmic reticulum,** or ER. Many cell substances are made in the ER. Proteins are made in small, circular structures called **ribosomes.** Proteins are released into the cell from the ER and the ribosomes by Golgi bodies. The Golgi bodies are flat, baglike structures that store and release chemicals from the cell. **Mitochondria** are rod-shaped structures in the cytoplasm that release energy for use in the cell.

Groups of similar cells that work together to perform a special job are **tissues.** Bone, muscle, blood, and nerve tissues are present in the human body. Bone tissue is made of bone cells. Muscle tissue is made of muscle cells. What are nerve tissues made of?

A group of tissues that work together to perform one or more life activities is an **organ.** The heart, eyes, brain, stomach, and lungs are a few of the organs in the human body. A **system** is a group of organs that work together to carry on life activities. The heart is a part of the circulatory system. The brain is a part of the nervous system. The digestive system is made of many organs, including the stomach and the mouth. ■

Lesson Review

Fill in the circle containing the letter of the term or phrase that correctly completes each statement.

1. _____ is the study of the jobs performed by various parts of the human body.
   (a) Anatomy   (b) Physiology   (c) Nucleus   (d) ER

2. Cells _____.
   (a) change food into energy   (b) dispose of wastes   (c) reproduce   (d) all of the above

3. The _____ controls the activities of a cell.
   (a) blood   (b) ER   (c) nucleus   (d) mitochondria

4. Proteins are made in the _____ of cells.
   (a) ER   (b) nucleus   (c) chromosomes   (d) ribosomes

5. A(n) _____ is a group of similar cells that work together.
   (a) tissue   (b) organ   (c) system   (d) chromosome

6. A group of tissues that work together to perform one or more life activities is a(n) _____.
   (a) tissue   (b) organ   (c) system   (d) chromosome

7. A(n) _____ is a group of organs that work together to carry on life activities.
   (a) tissue   (b) organ   (c) system   (d) chromosome

8. A nerve in your finger is a(n) _____.
   (a) tissue   (b) organ   (c) system   (d) chromosome

● 9. The movement of water into a cell is controlled by the _____.
   (a) ER   (b) cytoplasm   (c) cell membrane   (d) organ

● 10. Blood is a part of the _____ system.
   (a) circulatory   (b) digestive   (c) nervous   (d) none of the above

The Circulatory System

The human circulatory system moves, or circulates, blood throughout the body. The major parts of the system are the heart, the blood vessels, and the blood. The system is powered by the **heart,** a strong, muscular, four-chambered pump. The heart lies near the center of the chest and extends toward the left side of the body. In an adult, the heart and the fist, which grow at nearly the same rate, are about the same size.

The upper chambers of the heart are the right **atrium** and the left atrium. The lower chambers are the right and left **ventricles.** The opening between the atrium and the ventricle on each side of the heart is called a valve. Valves allow the blood to flow in only one direction. The pressure needed to pump blood through the circulatory system is provided by the heart muscles, which alternately contract and relax. The right side of the heart takes in blood from the body and pumps it to the lungs. The left side of the heart takes in blood from the lungs and pumps it to the body.

Blood is carried to and from the heart in tubes called blood vessels. There are three kinds of blood vessels. Blood vessels that carry blood to the heart are **veins.** Blood vessels that carry blood away from the heart are **arteries. Capillaries** are tiny blood vessels that connect veins and arteries.

How does blood move through your body? Blood enters the heart through the right atrium, the upper-right chamber. It is then pumped downward to the right ventricle and leaves the heart through the arteries which carry it to the lungs. In the lungs, carbon dioxide is removed from the blood and oxygen is added. Blood leaving the lungs enters the left atrium and passes downward through the left ventricle. Here it is pumped into a large artery called the aorta, which carries blood

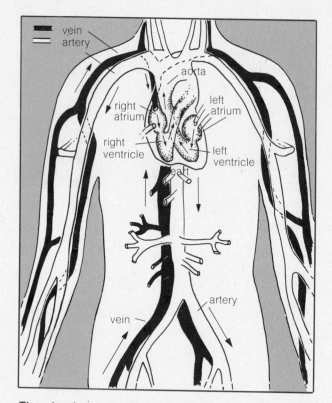

The circulatory system transports blood through the human body.

to the rest of the body. Eventually, blood flows into the capillaries in all organs and tissues of the body. Finally, the blood is carried by veins back to the right atrium.

Blood is tissue composed of plasma, red blood cells, white blood cells, and platelets. **Plasma,** a clear, watery fluid, makes up about 55 percent of a person's total blood supply. Nutrients such as oxygen and compounds of sodium, calcium, potassium, and magnesium are found in plasma. Plasma also contains substances that protect against diseases.

Red blood cells are cells in the plasma that carry oxygen. They contain a substance called hemoglobin, which contains iron and protein and gives blood its reddish color. Red blood cells make up about 44 percent of blood. **White blood cells** are produced in bone marrow, lymph nodes, and the spleen. White blood cells protect the body against infection. White blood cells can leave the bloodstream to fight organisms that cause disease. The white blood cells either destroy the organisms or are killed in the battle.

Platelets are tiny, colorless structures in blood that help blood to clot.

What does blood do? When food is taken into the body, it is changed into a form that the body can use. Blood carries food and oxygen to tissues in the body and removes wastes and excess water from these tissues. Blood carries carbon dioxide from the body tissues to the lungs. ■

Lesson Review

On the line before each statement, write the letter of the choice that best completes the statement.

_____ 1. The circulatory system is powered by the _____.

    a. veins   b. arteries   c. blood   d. heart

_____ 2. _____ allow blood to flow only in one direction.

    a. Veins   b. Valves   c. Arteries   d. Capillaries

_____ 3. Blood vessels that carry blood to the heart are _____.

    a. veins   b. capillaries   c. arteries   d. all of the above

_____ 4. Blood enters the heart through the _____.

    a. right atrium   b. right ventricle   c. left atrium   d. left ventricle

_____ 5. In the lungs, _____ the blood.

    a. carbon dioxide is removed from   c. plasma is added to

    b. oxygen is removed from   d. plasma is removed from

_____ 6. _____ are cells that protect the body against infection.

    a. Red blood cells   b. White blood cells   c. Platelets   d. Plasma

_____ 7. Tiny, colorless structures in blood that help it clot are _____.

    a. red blood cells   b. white blood cells   c. platelets   d. plasma

_____ 8. Blood carries _____.

    a. food and oxygen to body tissues   c. wastes into cells and tissues

    b. carbon dioxide from the lungs   d. all of the above

● _____ 9. One percent of blood by volume is made of _____.

    a. plasma   c. white blood cells

    b. plasma and red blood cells   d. platelets and white blood cells

● _____ 10. A person with fewer white blood cells than normal is more likely to _____.

    a. eat more   c. have a heart attack

    b. get an infection   d. suffer serious bleeding

The Digestive System

All animals, including humans, must eat food in order to survive. The food that is eaten by animals, however, is not in a form that the body can use. The process that changes food into usable forms is digestion. Digestion takes place in the digestive system, which is made up of the digestive tract and other organs. The **digestive tract** is a long tube through which food passes. It includes the mouth, esophagus, stomach, small intestine, large intestine, and anus. The liver and the pancreas aid digestion but are not parts of the digestive tract.

What happens to the food you eat? Digestion begins in the mouth. Teeth tear and grind food into small particles. These particles are moved by the tongue and mixed with saliva from the salivary glands. Saliva adds water and mucus to food so that it can be easily swallowed. Saliva contains an enzyme that aids in breaking down starches. An **enzyme** is a substance that speeds up the rate of a chemical reaction. Digestive enzymes are found in the mouth, the stomach, and the small intestine.

When food is swallowed, it passes into the **esophagus,** a tube that connects the mouth with the stomach. A little flap called the epiglottis then automatically closes to prevent the food that is swallowed from entering the lungs. The food is pushed by muscles in the esophagus into the stomach. The reflex muscle motion that causes the food to move from the esophagus to the stomach and on through the rest of the digestive system is known as **peristalsis.**

Once in the stomach, the food is mixed with gastric juices. Gastric juices are about 99 percent water, and they also contain hydrochloric acid and enzymes. Gastric juices begin the chemical digestion of proteins. Stomach muscles contract and relax to physically churn and mix the food with the gastric juices. This mixture remains in the stomach from three to five hours before it passes into the small intestine.

The **small intestine** is a coiled tube about 20 feet long in which most chemical digestion takes place. Intestinal juice, pancreatic juice, and bile are three digestive juices in the small intestine. Intestinal juice contains enzymes that digest carbohydrates, fats, and proteins. Pancreatic juice contains enzymes that digest starches, fats, and proteins. Bile does not contain enzymes but aids in breaking down fats.

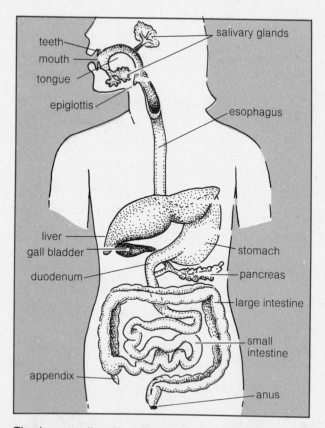

teeth
mouth
tongue
epiglottis
salivary glands
esophagus
liver
gall bladder
duodenum
stomach
pancreas
large intestine
small intestine
appendix
anus

The human digestive tract includes the mouth, esophagus, stomach, small and large intestines, and anus.

Digested food diffuses, or spreads out, into the blood through the walls of the small intestine. The lining of the small intestine is covered with small, fingerlike projections called **villi.** Villi contain blood that takes in the digested food from the intestine.

The food that is not digested or diffused into the blood collects in the large intestine.

The **large intestine,** which is a coiled tube that is about five feet long when uncoiled, is an organ that removes excess water from undigested food. The large intestine also secretes mucus that smooths the passage of wastes out of the body. Wastes leave the body through the anus. ■

Digestion	
mouth	Teeth grind food. Saliva moistens food.
esophagus	Food is carried to the stomach.
stomach	Gastric juices begin the chemical digestion of food.
small intestine	Intestinal juice, pancreatic juice, and bile complete chemical digestion of food. Blood in the villi takes in the digested food and carries it throughout the body.
large intestine	Waste is carried out of the body.

Lesson Review

In the space before each number, write the letter of the word or group of words in Column 2 that matches the description in Column 1.

Column 1

_____ 1. includes the mouth, esophagus, stomach, small and large intestines, and anus

_____ 2. a substance that speeds up a chemical reaction in the body

_____ 3. tube connecting the mouth with the stomach

_____ 4. muscle motion that causes food to move through the digestive tract

_____ 5. a coiled tube in which chemical digestion occurs

_____ 6. aids in the breakdown of fats

_____ 7. diffuses into the blood through the wall of the small intestine

_____ 8. fingerlike projections that line the small intestine

● _____ 9. organ that produces digestive juices used in the small intestine

● _____ 10. carries solid waste to the anus

Column 2

a. bile

b. digested food

c. digestive tract

d. enzyme

e. esophagus

f. large intestine

g. pancreas

h. peristalsis

i. small intestine

j. villi

Lesson 4

The Respiratory System

Recall that oxygen makes up about 21 percent of Earth's air. People can live only a few minutes without this gas. Oxygen used by humans and other animals is taken in by the respiratory system. The human respiratory system has five major parts: the nose, the mouth, the trachea, the lungs, and the diaphragm.

Normal breathing is done through the nose. Air enters the openings, or nostrils, in the nose. It then passes through tubes called the nasal passages. The nasal passages are lined with a soft, moist membrane. Tiny hairs called **cilia** line the membrane. Cilia remove dust, pollen, and other particles from the air. What happens when a person breathes through the mouth?

After air enters either the nose or the mouth, it may pass toward the larynx. The **larynx,** or voice box, is made of cartilage and contains the vocal cords. Air passing between the vocal cords causes them to vibrate. The vibrating vocal cords and movements of the tongue and mouth are used when people speak.

During normal breathing, incoming air bypasses the larynx and enters the trachea. The **trachea** is the tube that carries air to the lungs. The trachea branches into two tubes called bronchi. Each bronchus leads to a lung. Within the lungs, the bronchi branch out into small **bronchial tubes.** Bronchial tubes are made of even smaller microscopic tubes called bronchioles. Bronchioles are connected to tiny air sacs, or **alveoli.** A network of capillaries surrounds each alveolus. The lungs are made of millions of alveoli. Oxygen from the air diffuses through the alveoli and enters the blood through the thin walls of the capillaries. There the oxygen attaches to the hemoglobin of red blood cells and is transported

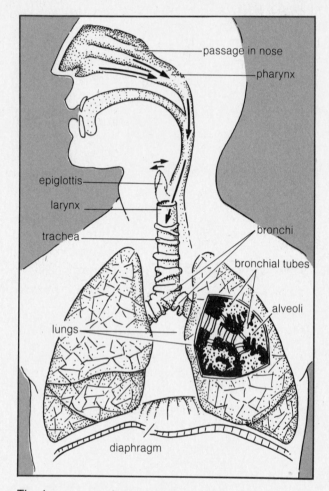

The human respiratory system includes the nose, mouth, trachea, lungs, and diaphragm.

throughout the body. Carbon dioxide, a waste product of cells, diffuses from the blood into the alveoli. Carbon dioxide is pushed out of the body when people exhale or breathe out. An outer membrane called the pleura protects the lungs from rubbing against the ribs or other parts of the chest cavity during breathing.

The **diaphragm** is a strong sheet of muscles beneath the lungs that contracts and relaxes during breathing. When relaxed, the diaphragm is dome-shaped. During inhalation, the diaphragm flattens and the ribs move outward. This causes an increase in the volume of the chest cavity and a decrease in air pressure. Air rushes in through the nose or mouth to fill the lungs. During exhalation, the diaphragm domes upward and the ribs move inward. This decreases the volume of the chest cavity. Therefore, air is forced out of the nose or mouth.

The main functions of the respiratory system are breathing, supplying the blood with oxygen, and removing carbon dioxide from the blood. An exchange of gases takes place during breathing. Inhaled air is about 21 percent oxygen, 78 percent nitrogen, and less than one percent carbon dioxide. Exhaled air contains about 16 percent oxygen, 78 percent nitrogen, and about four percent carbon dioxide.

Respiration is the process by which oxygen is combined with food, and energy is released. During respiration, oxygen from the air enters the lungs and diffuses into the blood. The blood then carries the oxygen throughout the body, where it diffuses into the body's cells. In the cells, oxygen combines with a form of sugar called glucose, and energy is released. Carbon dioxide, which is a waste product of the reaction, diffuses into the blood and is disposed of through exhalation. ■

Lesson Review

In the space provided, write the word or words that best complete the statement.

1. Normal breathing occurs through the _____.

2. _____ line the membrane of the nose and filter some of the particles from the air.

3. Vibrating vocal cords and _____ are used when people speak.

4. The _____ transports air to the lungs.

5. Bronchioles are connected to tiny air sacs called _____.

6. The outer membrane, or _____, protects the lungs from rubbing against the ribs or other parts of the chest cavity.

7. During inhalation, the diaphragm _____ and the ribs move outward.

8. Air in the chest cavity is _____ during exhalation.

● 9. A person who is exercising needs more oxygen than someone at rest. Deep breathing by the person exercising _____ the carbon dioxide level.

● 10. The lungs are elastic tissue that cannot expand or contract on their own. The _____ is responsible for the expansion and contraction of the lungs.

The Nervous System and the Eye

The human nervous system allows us to see, hear, speak, touch, taste, think, and move. Nerves carry messages back and forth between the brain and the rest of the body. In humans, the **central nervous system** includes the brain and the spinal cord. The brain is the major control center of the body. The spinal cord is a thick bundle of nerves that extends from the base of the brain to the base of the spine. The **peripheral nervous system** is made up of all other nerves.

The basic building block of the nervous system is the nerve cell, or **neuron.** Neurons carry impulses, or messages, throughout the body. A neuron is made of three parts: a cell body, dendrites, and an axon. The **cell body** contains the cytoplasm, a nucleus, and other parts of the cell. **Dendrites** are extensions of the cell body that receive stimuli. The **axon** is a branching tube that extends from the cell body and carries impulses from the cell body to the next neuron.

In humans, there are three kinds of neurons: sensory neurons, interneurons, and motor neurons. Sensory neurons carry messages to the central nervous system. Interneurons connect sensory neurons and motor neurons. Motor neurons carry impulses away from the central nervous system.

What happens when you touch the end of a hot cooking pot? The neurons in your finger are stimulated. An impulse is sent along sensory neurons to the central nervous system. Interneurons transfer the impulse from the sensory neurons to the motor neurons. The motor neurons send nerve impulses to the muscles in your hand. The muscles contract, and you pull your hand away from the hot pot. Since impulses travel at speeds of up to 400 feet per second, all this has occurred even before you are aware of the heat!

Pulling your hand away from a hot pot is an involuntary reaction. It happens without thinking. In most simple reflex acts, the brain is not involved. More complex reflex actions and voluntary movements, however, are controlled by the brain. Walking, swimming, and running are voluntary movements.

The five senses of sight, hearing, touch, taste, and smell are controlled by the brain. All vertebrates have two eyes that are able to detect light and change it into nerve messages. Light enters the human eye through the **cornea,** a transparent covering which protects the front portion of the eye. Under the cornea is an opening called the **pupil.** The pupil is surrounded by the **iris**, or colored part of the eye. Muscles in the iris control the amount of light that enters the eye. In bright light, the iris gets larger and the pupil becomes smaller. What happens to the pupil in a darkened room?

The **lens**, which is located behind the iris, focuses light rays on the back surface of the eye called the **retina.** The retina is attached to the optic nerve. The optic nerve carries messages from the eye to the brain. A blind spot exists where the optic nerve joins the retina.

What happens when you look at something? Light enters the cornea where it is refracted, or bent. The light then passes through the lens, which focuses the light on the retina. The retina changes the light rays into signals. These signals are carried by the optic nerve to the brain where they are interpreted as images.

If the image focused on the retina is not clear and sharp, there may be a defect in the eye. Nearsightedness, or myopia, occurs when a person can see close objects clearly, but distant objects appear fuzzy. Farsighted

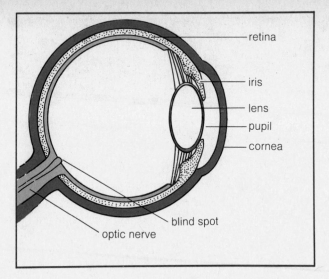

The eye is a sense organ of the nervous system.

vision, or hyperopia, occurs when a person sees distant objects clearly, but close objects appear fuzzy. Another common visual problem is astigmatism. In this condition, a distorted lens and corneal surface do not allow the light rays that enter the eye to focus sharply on the retina. People with astigmatism often see blurred images of both close and distant objects. Glasses and contact lenses can help to correct myopia, hyperopia, and astigmatism.

Strabismus is an eye defect in which the eyes are not used together. One eye is often turned either too far toward the nose or too far from the nose. Strabismus often affects children, sometimes causing them to have blurred or double vision. If detected early, strabismus may be corrected with glasses, medication, eye surgery, or a patch worn over one eye.

Colorblindness is another eye defect. People with red-green colorblindness cannot distinguish between red and green. In another form of colorblindness, green is seen as gray and red is seen as yellow. Colorblindness is a sex-linked trait. A sex-linked trait is a trait controlled by genes on one or the other sex chromosome. About eight percent of American males are colorblind. Less than one-half of one percent of American females are colorblind. ■

Lesson Review

Determine whether each of the following statements is true or false. Correct each false statement by crossing out the word or phrase that makes it false and by writing the correct word or phrase above it.

_____ 1. The peripheral nervous system includes the brain and the spinal cord.

_____ 2. Neurons carry impulses or messages throughout the body.

_____ 3. Dendrites carry impulses from the cell body to the next neuron.

_____ 4. Sensory neurons carry messages to the central nervous system.

_____ 5. The brain is involved in most involuntary reflex acts.

_____ 6. Light rays enter the human eye through the cornea.

_____ 7. Muscles in the lens control the amount of light that enters the eye.

_____ 8. People with astigmatism see blurred images of both close and distant objects.

● _____ 9. A boy is more likely to be colorblind than a girl.

● _____ 10. Riding a bike is an involuntary movement.

If you are in a closed room and somebody makes a loud sound in a nearby room, you are probably able to hear the sound. The sound travels through the floor, the walls, and the air to your ears. Your ears collect the sound waves and transmit them to the brain as nerve impulses. The brain records these impulses as music, human speech, or other sound.

Sound is a wave, or rhythmic disturbance of air, that carries energy. Sound waves are produced by vibrating matter. The human ear can distinguish over 300,000 different sounds. Most people can hear sounds with wave frequencies between about 20 hertz and 20,000 hertz. **Frequency** is the number of waves that pass a given point in one second. One hertz is equal to one wave per second.

Ultrasounds are sounds with frequencies above 20,000 hertz. Many animals can hear ultrasounds. Most dog whistles, for example, can produce sounds between 20,000 and 25,000 hertz. People are unable to hear ultrasounds.

Sounds can be as soft as a whisper or as loud as a jet engine. The intensity of a sound depends upon the height of the sound wave. A loud sound produces a sound wave with a large wave height. Loudness is measured in units called decibels, which are abbreviated dB. Whispers range from 15 to 20 decibels. Most lawn mowers reach about 100 dB. When the loudness is greater than about 120 dB, people feel pain. The loudness of a jet engine when a plane is taking off can exceed 150 dB.

How do people hear sound? The ear has three main parts: the outer ear, the middle ear, and the inner ear. The outer ear is the visible tissue on the side of your head.

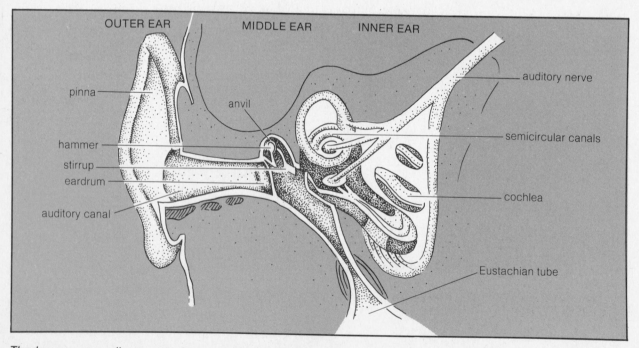

The human ear collects sound waves and transmits them to the brain.

The outer ear collects sound waves. The waves are then channeled through the **auditory canal,** a tube that amplifies the waves and protects the inner ear from dust, water, and changes in temperature. The auditory canal is about one inch in length. The auditory canal leads to the **eardrum,** a thin sheet of tissue that separates the outer ear from the middle ear. When sound waves hit the eardrum, it vibrates. The vibrations are carried to three tiny bones in the middle ear: the hammer, the anvil, and the stirrup.

The **eustachian tube** connects the middle ear with the throat. This tube allows air to flow into and out of the middle ear to equalize air pressure on both sides of the eardrum. A rapid change in elevation often causes a pressure imbalance on the eardrum. People sometimes experience this kind of pressure imbalance when a plane is taking off or landing. Pressure can be equalized by yawning or swallowing. This causes your ears to "pop" as the eustachian tube opens and allows air either to enter or leave the middle ear.

The hammer, anvil, and stirrup connect the eardrum to a structure in the inner ear called the **cochlea** that is shaped like a snail. The cochlea is filled with fluid that vibrates when sound waves are sent from the middle ear. This movement stimulates hairlike cells in the inner ear. The hairlike cells send the nerve impulses to the **auditory nerve,** which transmits the signals to the brain. The brain interprets these impulses as the sounds you hear.

The inner ear also has canals that give you balance. The semicircular canals are tubes filled with fluid. The fluid moves as you move your body or your head. This stimulates the nerves in the tubes to send impulses to the brain. The brain translates these signals and helps you to keep your balance. ∎

Lesson Review

In the space before each number, write the letter of the word or group of words in Column 2 that matches the description in Column 1.

Column 1

_____ 1. rhythmic disturbance of air that carries energy

_____ 2. number of waves that pass a given point in one second

_____ 3. visible tissue on the side of the head that gathers sound waves

_____ 4. tube that amplifies sound waves that enter the ear

_____ 5. one of three bones in the middle ear

_____ 6. thin sheet of tissue that separates the outer ear from the middle ear

_____ 7. tube that connects the middle ear to the throat

_____ 8. structure that sends nerve impulses to the brain

• _____ 9. device for changing the height of certain sound waves

• _____ 10. minor ear problem that can be caused by a fast descent down a mountain

Column 2

a. auditory canal

b. auditory nerve

c. eardrum

d. eustachian tube

e. frequency

f. hammer

g. outer ear

h. pressure imbalance

i. radio volume control

j. sound

The Reproductive System

Reproduction, or the production of offspring, allows a species to survive. People are mammals. Mammals reproduce by the internal fertilization of a female egg by a male sperm to produce a zygote. The zygote grows into an embryo that develops with time into a new organism inside the female's body.

The human female reproductive system produces eggs in sex organs called **ovaries.** Females have two ovaries, which are found in the lower abdominal cavity. At birth, the ovaries contain about two million egg cells. Only about 400 of these eggs, however, will mature by adulthood. Egg cells do not begin to mature until the female reaches puberty. **Puberty** is a time when humans are first able to reproduce.

Once puberty begins, an egg is released from the ovary into an oviduct, or fallopian tube, in the process of **ovulation.** Generally, only one egg is released each month. Ovulation alternates monthly between the two ovaries. Ovulation usually takes place about 14 days before the onset of menstruation. **Menstruation** is a process during which blood and other tissues necessary for reproduction are shed from the uterus through the vagina. The **uterus** is a hollow organ about the size of a pear. It has a narrow opening, or cervix, that leads to the vagina. The **vagina** is a canal that leads to the outside of the female's body.

The **menstrual cycle,** or female reproductive cycle, averages 28 days. The menstrual cycle involves the maturation of the egg in the ovary. This is followed by ovulation. For about 48 hours before and 48 hours after ovulation, a female can become pregnant if sperm are in the fallopian tubes. As the egg moves into the uterus, the lining of the uterus thickens. If the egg is not fertilized, the tissues in the uterus break down and menstrua-tion occurs. Menstruation usually lasts between four and six days. The cycle then begins again. Females menstruate until the age of about 45 to 55.

Unlike the reproductive organs in human females, which are internal, the human male's reproductive organs are mostly outside the body. Sperm are produced in coiled tubes inside the two oval-shaped glands called the **testes.** Production of sperm begins at puberty and continues through male adulthood. The testes produce sperm at a rate of between ten billion to 30 billion per month. The testes are enclosed in a sac called the **scrotum.**

Millions of sperm are released from the testes during ejaculation. The sperm then pass

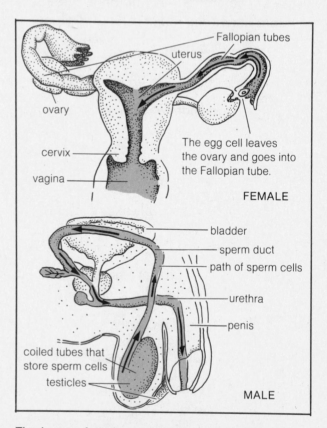

The human female reproductive organs are internal whereas the male organs are mostly external.

through a series of glands that produce a whitish fluid. The fluid combines with the sperm to form **semen.** Contractions of the glands force semen through a tube in the penis. Semen passes out of the body through the urethra, a tube that connects the bladder to the penis.

During intercourse, millions of sperm cells enter the vagina. Each sperm has a head and a tail. The tail whips back and forth to move the sperm through the uterus and into the fallopian tubes. Millions of sperm are released, yet it takes only one sperm to fertilize an egg.

Fertilization produces a zygote. As the zygote moves into the uterus, the zygote divides to form an embryo. Once the embryo enters the uterus, it attaches itself to the uterine wall. By the ninth week, the embryo develops into a fetus. A fetus grows and matures in the uterus. The entire process from fertilization to birth lasts about 266 days. During pregnancy, the uterus grows to many times its usual size. During **labor,** or the beginning of childbirth, the muscles in the uterus contract involuntarily for hours to help to push the baby out of the mother's body through the vagina. ■

Lesson Review

Fill in the circle containing the letter of the term or phrase that correctly completes each statement.

1. The human female produces eggs in sex organs called _____.
   - (a) vaginas
   - (b) ovaries
   - (c) testes
   - (d) urethras

2. The time at which humans are first able to reproduce is _____.
   - (a) ovulation
   - (b) labor
   - (c) menstruation
   - (d) puberty

3. _____ is the process by which an egg cell is released into a fallopian tube.
   - (a) Ovulation
   - (b) Puberty
   - (c) Labor
   - (d) Menstruation

4. The _____ is a canal that leads to the outside of a female's body.
   - (a) vagina
   - (b) cervix
   - (c) fallopian tube
   - (d) uterus

5. The menstrual cycle averages about _____.
   - (a) 48 hours
   - (b) 14 days
   - (c) 28 days
   - (d) 266 days

6. Sperm are produced in the _____.
   - (a) urethra
   - (b) penis
   - (c) bladder
   - (d) testes

7. The testes are enclosed in a sac called the _____.
   - (a) bladder
   - (b) scrotum
   - (c) uterus
   - (d) none of the above

8. Semen is a white fluid that also contains _____.
   - (a) egg cells
   - (b) urine
   - (c) sperm cells
   - (d) all of the above

● 9. Human females no longer ovulate after _____.
   - (a) puberty begins
   - (c) menstruation ceases
   - (b) adolescence ends
   - (d) adulthood begins

● 10. A developing fetus receives nourishment from the _____.
   - (a) vagina
   - (b) uterus
   - (c) cervix
   - (d) testes

Organ Transplants

In 1967, the world was astounded at the news that a surgical team, headed by Dr. Christiaan Barnard, had transplanted a whole human heart. A transplant involves the removal of a body part, often an organ, from one person, and the placement of that body part into another person. The survival rate for early heart transplant patients was not very high. This was mainly due to the fact that the recipient's body often rejected the transplanted organ. Most early patients lived less than a year after surgery. The survival rate of heart transplant patients increased dramatically in the early 1980s.

Today, transplants of hearts and other human organs are becoming almost routine procedures. This is good news for thousands of people who are in need of a replacement organ. In the early part of 1989, patients on waiting lists for transplants of major organs numbered almost 17,000. Nearly 15,000 of these patients needed a kidney. The second largest group, which included about 1,200 people, were potential heart recipients. The remaining patients were on lists for liver, heart/lung, pancreas, and lung transplants.

Unfortunately, there are not enough organs to meet the demand. Organs must be donated to organ banks, which are organizations that match donated organs to those who need them. Strict laws allow the much needed organs to be taken only when a donating person has been diagnosed as being brain dead. A brain dead person is one whose brain shows no activity and whose body cannot breathe unassisted. Potential organs are kept healthy by machines that pump oxygen to the lungs and circulate blood in the body of a brain-dead person.

Due to the shortage of organ donors and the problems associated with transplants, machines are sometimes used to temporarily replace or assist a damaged organ. A dialysis machine, for example, does the work of the kidneys, thereby helping the body to function as

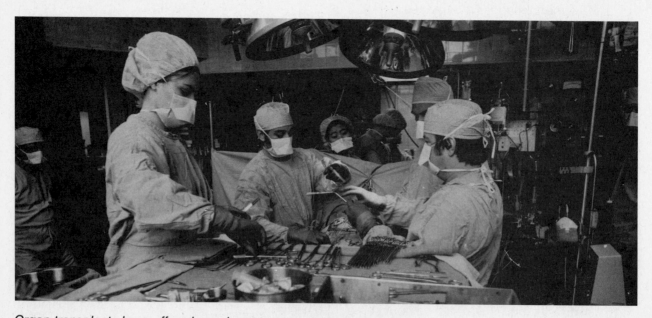

Organ transplants have offered new hope to many critically-ill patients.

normally as possible. A pacemaker regulates the heartbeat. A device called an assisting heart can take over for a failing left ventricle until it recovers and can pump enough blood on its own. In 1982, the first permanent artificial heart was implanted in a patient, Barney Clark. He lived for 112 days.

Perhaps in the future, people in need of organs will be able to rely on artificial organs. For now, however, their greatest hope lies with organs donated by living and deceased persons. Of the estimated 25,000 suitable organ donors annually, fewer than 17 percent choose to donate organs. In an attempt to increase the number of donors, federal laws were passed in 1987 that require hospitals to ask survivors for permission to use organs that are suitable for transplants. Unfortunately, these efforts have not produced a significant increase in the number of organs donated.

Organ transplants raise a number of questions. Who should pay for the cost of the surgery? Should the most critically-ill patients receive organs? Or should the organs go to healthier persons who may have better chances of survival? Should a patient whose body rejected an organ be given another organ? Information about organ transplants can be obtained from the American Council on Transplantation. ∎

Lesson Review

Identify each of the following statements as true or false. Correct each false statement by crossing out the word or phrase that makes it false and by writing the correct word or phrase above it.

_____ 1. The survival rate for early heart transplant patients was very high.

_____ 2. Most transplant recipients are in need of a heart.

_____ 3. Organ banks are organizations that match donated organs to potential patients.

_____ 4. A brain-dead person is one whose brain shows no activity.

_____ 5. A dialysis machine regulates heartbeat.

_____ 6. Few people today rely on organs donated by living and deceased people.

_____ 7. Special laws have produced a significant increase in the number of donated organs.

_____ 8. A brain-dead person is able to breathe without assistance.

● _____ 9. About 88 percent of the patients on waiting lists for transplants of major organs were potential kidney recipients.

● _____ 10. Early artificial heart recipients lived for a shorter period of time than later heart-transplant recipients.

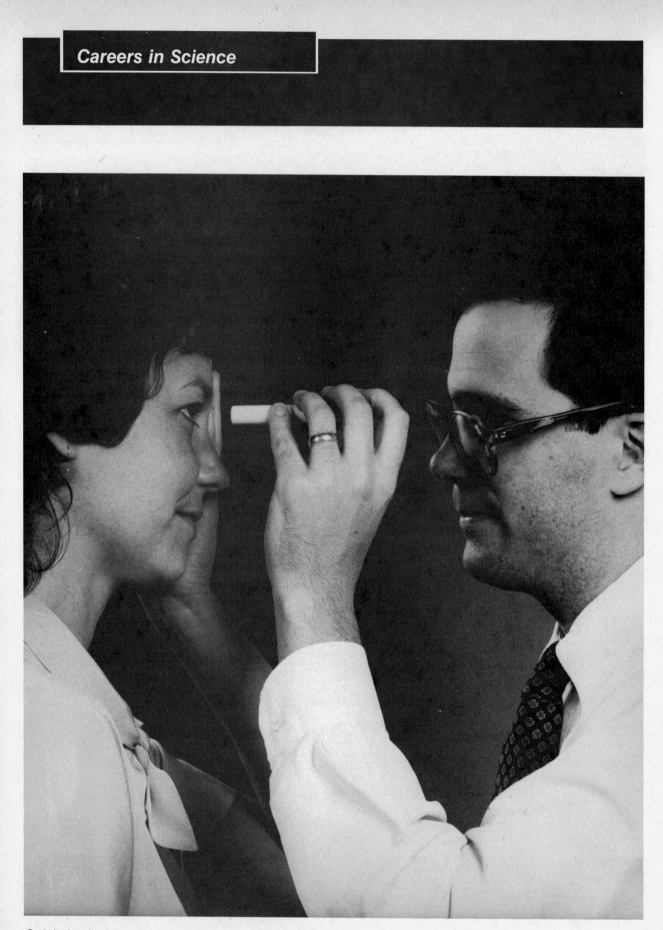

Ophthalmologists care for and treat conditions of the eyes.

Physicians work to preserve and restore human health. Physicians examine patients, diagnose problems, and develop treatment strategies. Many physicians specialize in a particular branch of medicine that treats only one system of the body. Many physicians are in private practice. Others belong to clinics or practice groups who share the same specialty. Some physicians do research and teach. Physicians also work for branches of government that have a responsibility for public health.

Emergency medical technicians are trained medical workers who provide certain kinds of medical treatment in emergency situations. All emergency medical technicians, or EMTs, provide first-aid and basic life support. Paramedics, who have more training than EMTs, can administer drugs and supply advanced procedures under the radio control of a physician at a nearby hospital. Most emergency medical technicians work for local fire departments. Some work for hospitals and private ambulance services.

Pathologists study the causes and effects of diseases in the human body. A pathologist studies the changes that occur when a disease strikes tissues, organs, or cells. Pathologists often teach and do research at medical schools and universities. Some pathologists work for government agencies that are engaged in public health, agriculture, and law enforcement. As a matter of fact, many coroners are pathologists. Private companies in the chemical and drug industries often employ pathologists to help guide teams of other scientists who work on developing new products.

Pharmacists fill prescriptions that physicians write for their patients. They prepare labels for the medicines that include all of the information that the patient needs to take the prescription correctly. Pharmacists also advise people about nonprescription drugs, such as cold tablets and cough mixtures. Some pharmacists work in medical centers and research laboratories. Many work in retail drug stores. A large number of pharmacists own and operate their own drug stores.

Ophthalmologists specialize in caring for and treating conditions of the eyes. They conduct vision examinations and, based on the results of these exams, sometimes prescribe glasses and contact lenses. Some ophthalmologists are in private practice. Others teach and do research at colleges and universities. Ophthalmologists often employ optometrists. Optometrists are specialists who are licensed to conduct eye exams and prescribe corrective lenses or necessary exercises. Some optometrists own and operate their own businesses.

Laboratory technicians and medical assistants work in all fields of human anatomy and physiology. Physicians' assistants and nurses' associates help physicians to provide direct medical care. A wide variety of people with the appropriate technical background provide services in laboratories, museums, hospitals, and physicians' offices. ∎

For Further Information

More information about these and related careers is available from the following publications and organizations.

Careers in Health Care, Rachel Epstein, Chelsea House, 1989

Your Future in Medical Technology, Richards Rosen Press, 1978

American Medical Technologists
710 Higgins Road
Park Ridge, IL 60068

American Optometric Association
243 Lindbergh Boulevard
St. Louis, MO 63141

American Association of Pathologists
9650 Rockville Pike
Bethesda, MD 20814

American Medical Association
535 N. Dearborn Street
Chicago, IL 60610

Health

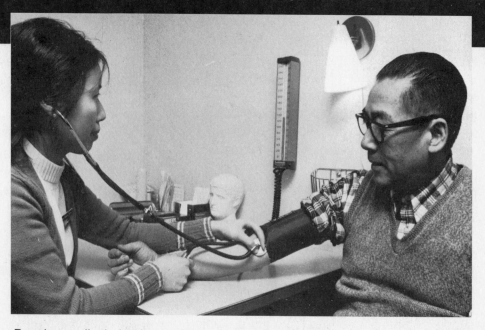

Regular medical checkups help to maintain good health.

Lesson 1

Basic Needs

Good health leads to physical and mental well being. Healthy people generally feel good and function well. The most important aspect of good health is proper nutrition. **Nutrition** is the study of food and its use by the human body. **Nutrients,** or substances needed by the body for life activities, include water, minerals, carbohydrates, fats, proteins, and vitamins. Exercise, rest, good personal hygiene, and medical and dental care are also essential to good health.

The human body is between 60 and 70 percent water. Therefore, water is one of the most important nutrients needed by the body. In fact, the human body can exist without food for at least one month, but it can only go without water for a few days. The body uses water to break down foods. Water then carries the other nutrients provided by food to various parts of the body via the blood. Water also helps to carry wastes from the body. Urine and perspiration are mostly water. A person needs about two-and-a-half quarts of water each day.

In addition to proper nutrition, exercise is important to good health. Exercise strengthens muscles and improves the efficiency of the circulatory and respiratory systems. Walking, bicycling, jogging, and swimming are a few forms of exercise that lead to a healthy body. To receive the most benefits from an exercise program, a person should begin gradually. An exercise program should begin slowly and build up to a level that will maintain strong muscles and a healthy heart. Ideally, a person should exercise four or five days a week, varying the kind of exercise done daily. It has been shown that a once-a-week, vigorous activity such as handball is of little benefit and may even harm someone who is out of shape.

Everyone needs sleep, but the amount of

sleep needed varies from person to person. Most adults sleep from seven to eight hours per day. Young children may need ten or more hours of sleep each day. When a person sleeps, the body relaxes. Life processes slow down. Sleep restores energy needed by the body. After a good night's sleep, the body is refreshed.

Rest and relaxation are as important to the human body as sleep. Activities that differ from the normal work or study routine provide a change of pace and help to relieve tension.

Personal hygiene enhances overall health. Regular care of skin, hair, nails, and teeth can prevent disease and the transmission of certain diseases. **Skin** is a body organ that regulates temperature and provides a barrier against certain diseases. A daily bath or shower removes dirt, oils, bacteria, and perspiration from the outer layer of skin. Hair and nails should be trimmed regularly.

Nearly 95 percent of adults in the United States will experience some gum disease in their lifetimes. Good dental hygiene is essential to a healthy mouth. **Plaque,** a sticky material that forms on teeth within 20 minutes after eating, is harmful to dental health. Brushing and flossing teeth can remove plaque and stop it from forming on teeth.

Regular dental and medical care are essential ingredients of good personal hygiene. In addition to checkups on a regular basis, children are **immunized** or given medication to protect them against certain diseases, as a part of their health program. When any illness strikes, it is usually best to seek prompt medical and dental care. Self-diagnosis and delayed treatment can result in a longer period of illness and often increased cost. ■

Lesson Review

In the space before each number, write the letter of the word or group of words in Column 2 that matches the description in Column 1.

Column 1

_____ 1. the study of food and its use by the human body

_____ 2. water, minerals, fats, proteins, carbohydrates, and vitamins

_____ 3. makes up about 60 to 70 percent of the human body

_____ 4. maintains strong muscles and a healthy heart

_____ 5. need about seven to eight hours of sleep per day

_____ 6. regular care of skin, hair, nails, and teeth

_____ 7. a body organ that provides a barrier against certain diseases

_____ 8. a sticky material that forms on teeth within 20 minutes after eating

• _____ 9. a person doing this activity will breathe more slowly than when he or she is working

• _____ 10. a cut or scrape may make the body vulnerable to this

Column 2

a. most adults

b. disease

c. exercise

d. nutrients

e. nutrition

f. personal hygiene

g. plaque

h. skin

i. sleep

j. water

A Healthy Diet

It has been said that you are what you eat. Therefore, a healthy body must begin with a healthy diet. A healthy diet includes the essential nutrients needed for life activities. Recall that nutrients are substances needed by the body and include water, carbohydrates, fats, proteins, minerals, and vitamins.

A **carbohydrate** is an energy-rich compound made up of carbon, hydrogen, and oxygen. Carbohydrates, such as sugar and starch, are the body's main source of energy. A **Calorie** is a measure of the energy in foods. The number of Calories needed by a person depends on the person's age, sex, body structure, and activity level. The average adult needs about 2,500 Calories per day.

About 30 percent of the Calories in a well-balanced diet come from fats. Fats, like carbohydrates, are energy-rich compounds made of carbon, hydrogen, and oxygen. Butter, oils, cheese, milk, and nuts are sources of fats. Fats contain fatty acids that may be saturated or unsaturated. Saturated fatty acids contain as many hydrogen atoms as possible; unsaturated fatty acids contain fewer hydrogen atoms than usual. A diet of too many saturated fatty acids may raise the level of cholesterol. **Cholesterol** is a fat that has been linked with heart disease and other circulatory problems.

Minerals are elements found in nature that are needed in small amounts by the human body and include calcium, magnesium, phosphorous, iron, and iodine. Calcium, magnesium, and phosphorous are needed for strong bones and teeth. Milk and other dairy products are good sources of these minerals. Iron is needed by the body to form hemoglobin, a substance in blood. Liver, peas, egg yolks, and whole grains are rich in iron. Several glands in the body cannot function without iodine. Iodine is found in some seafood, milk, and iodized table salt.

Vitamins are organic compounds used by the body to regulate changes in the cells. Vitamins are needed only in small amounts and are found in the foods you eat. The names of some vitamins, information about them, and food sources of each are listed in the Table.

A balanced diet offers essential nutrients in the proper amounts. A balanced diet contains servings from the four basic food groups: the milk group, the meat group, the fruit-vegetable group, and the grain group. Some nutritionists often refer to a fifth group called combination foods. **Combination foods** are foods that include servings from the four basic food groups. A sausage pizza is a common combination food. ∎

Selected Vitamins

Vitamin	Needed for	Best Sources
A	Bones, teeth, eyesight	Milk, liver, butter, eggs, green and yellow vegetables
B_1 (Thiamine)	Digestion, energy, heart, nerves	Meat, cereal, nuts, vegetables
B_2 (Riboflavin)	Tissues, skin	Milk, cheese, fish, poultry, liver, green vegetables
B_3 (Niacin)	Tissues, energy, skin, nerves	Liver, meat, whole-grain or enriched cereals
C (Ascorbic acid)	Blood vessels, bones, teeth	Citrus fruits, raw cabbage, tomatoes, potatoes
D	Bones	Fatty fish, fortified milk, sunlight

The Four Food Groups

MILK-CHEESE GROUP

Children: 3–4 servings daily
Adults: 2 or more
servings daily

FRUIT-VEGETABLES
GROUP

4 or more servings daily

MEAT-POULTRY-FISH-
BEANS GROUP

2 or more
servings daily

GRAIN GROUP

4 or more servings daily

Lesson Review

On the line before each statement, write the letter of the choice that best completes the statement.

_____ 1. A(n) _____ is an energy-rich nutrient composed of carbon, hydrogen, and oxygen.

      a. vitamin   b. Calorie   c. carbohydrate   d. amino acid

_____ 2. The unit used to measure the amount of energy in food is a(n) _____.

      a. Calorie   b. fat   c. carbohydrate   d. cholesterol

_____ 3. A good source of fat is _____.

      a. butter   b. cheese   c. milk   d. all of the above

_____ 4. Saturated fats contain as many _____ atoms as possible.

      a. hydrogen   b. carbon   c. sulfur   d. oxygen

_____ 5. Cholesterol is a(n) _____ that has been linked with heart disease and other health problems.

      a. amino acid   b. mineral   c. protein   d. none of the above

_____ 6. Calcium is a _____.

      a. vitamin   b. fat   c. Calorie   d. mineral

_____ 7. _____ is needed by the blood to form hemoglobin.

      a. Calcium   b. Iodine   c. Iron   d. Magnesium

_____ 8. _____ are used by the body to regulate changes in cells.

      a. Vitamins   b. Fats   c. Minerals   d. Carbohydrates

● _____ 9. A well-balanced diet should include about _____ servings of meat daily.

      a. 1   b. 2   c. 5   d. 6

● _____ 10. The crust of a piece of pizza belongs to the _____ food group.

      a. milk   b. grain   c. meat   d. fruit-vegetable

Drugs

What do caffeine, cocaine, and aspirin all have in common? All are drugs. A **drug** is any substance, other than food, which can change life processes within the body. Some drugs combat disease. Other drugs relieve common illnesses. Some drugs, such as insulin, replace chemicals normally found in the body. Many drugs are able to help people lead more healthful lives. However, drugs can also be abused or improperly used.

How do drugs affect the body? Most drugs have more than one effect: the intended effect and side effects. A side effect of a drug is an unexpected or unintended effect. For example, many antihistamines are intended to relieve the symptoms of allergies but have the side effect of drowsiness. Some drugs are addictive, or habit-forming. **Physical addiction** is a condition in which the drug user must continue to take the drug in order to avoid withdrawal symptoms. **Psychological addiction** is the condition in which the drug user has developed an emotional need for the drug.

Medicines are drugs that are used to treat illnesses or diseases. Prescription drugs are medications that are ordered by a doctor for a patient. **Antibiotics** are prescription drugs used to combat bacteria. Meningitis, pneumonia, acne, and many infections are treated with antibiotics. Over-the-counter drugs are medicines that can be bought without a doctor's prescription. Aspirin and antihistamines are common over-the-counter drugs. Both prescription and over-the-counter drugs must be taken according to the instructions given.

Stimulants are drugs that increase the rate of the body's nervous system. Nicotine, caffeine, cocaine, and amphetamines are stimulants. Nicotine is found in tobacco products and can cause physical and psychological dependence. Caffeine is a mild stimulant that can cause psychological dependence. Caffeine is commonly found in many colas, teas, coffees, and in chocolate. Cocaine is a strong stimulant that comes from the leaves of the coca plant. All forms of cocaine, including crack, produce psychological dependence in users. Amphetamines are stimulants that also produce psychological dependence. Increases in heartbeat and blood pressure, restlessness, nervousness, rapid breathing, and loss of appetite are some effects of stimulants.

Depressants are drugs that decrease the activity of the nervous system. Tranquilizers, barbiturates, alcohol, and narcotics are depressants. Tranquilizers often are prescribed before surgery to reduce stress and relax muscles. Barbiturates are depressants that are sometimes prescribed by doctors for patients who are mentally ill to help them relax. The use of these drugs results in both psychological and physical dependence. Despite its acceptance

The abuse of alcohol can have fatal consequences.

by society, alcohol, like tobacco, is a dangerous drug. Alcohol is a depressant that is rapidly absorbed by the blood. Intoxication by alcohol leads to slurred speech, a loss in coordination, and a loss of judgment.

Narcotics are depressants that relieve pain and often cause drowsiness. Narcotics slow down the body's circulation and respiration. Narcotics also reduce blood pressure. Users of narcotics can become addicted to the drugs. Therefore, their use is strictly controlled. Withdrawal symptoms of users of narcotics include nervousness, hot and cold flashes, diarrhea, and stomach cramps. Common narcotics include morphine, codeine, and heroin. Morphine and codeine are derived from the opium poppy plant. Morphine is prescribed by doctors to relieve severe pain. Codeine is found in some prescription drugs and cough medicines. There is little medical use for heroin, an illegal drug often used by people addicted to narcotics.

Hallucinogens are drugs that cause users to imagine sights and sounds that do not exist. LSD, PCB, mescaline, and PCP are hallucinogens. These drugs are seldom used medically and often must be obtained illegally. The use of hallucinogens causes psychological and emotional changes that distort reality. The effects of some hallucinogens can recur long after their use has been discontinued.

Many drugs, including hormones and manufactured vitamins, help people to lead healthy lives. When drugs are taken as directed, many illnesses and diseases can be treated or prevented. The abuse of drugs, however, often leads to dependency. ∎

Lesson Review

In the space provided, write the word or words that best complete the statement.

1. A(n) _____ is any substance that can change life processes within the body.

2. Drugs that can be bought without a prescription are _____ drugs.

3. A(n) _____ of a drug is an unexpected or unintended effect.

4. _____ addiction is a condition in which the drug user has developed an emotional need for the drug.

5. Drugs often prescribed by doctors prior to surgery are _____.

6. Alcohol is a(n) _____ that is rapidly absorbed by the blood.

7. Codeine is a(n) _____ found in some prescription drugs and cough medicines.

8. The effects of some _____ can recur long after the use of the drugs has stopped.

● 9. Marijuana can increase the heartbeat rate by as much as 50 percent. Based on this information, marijuana can be classified as a(n) _____.

● 10. Weight-control drugs cause a loss of appetite. Weight-control drugs are _____.

Disease

Discoveries such as penicillin, insulin, and X rays have prevented and helped cure or control many diseases. A **disease** is a condition of the body or one of its parts that impairs the performance of the body or the body part. Diseases can be caused by viruses, bacteria, fungi, or protozoa.

A **virus** is a compound that has characteristics of both living and nonliving things. A virus is not made of cells, yet it can carry on life processes inside a living cell. Viruses can remain inactive for long periods of time outside or inside a cell. They may become active only when a cell is under stress or in a weakened condition. Currently, there are no drugs that can destroy viruses. Certain drugs can only be used to treat the symptoms of diseases caused by viruses. Many diseases are caused by viruses. Colds, AIDS, mumps, warts, the flu, chicken pox, measles, and perhaps some cancers are diseases caused by viruses.

Bacteria are one major group of the organisms called monerans. A bacterium has no nucleus, but it is able to reproduce. Most bacteria reproduce by dividing in half to form two new cells. Bacteria are found everywhere—in soil, in water, in air, on your skin, and in your body. Many bacteria are helpful. Some, such as those that cause tuberculosis, strep throat, and scarlet fever, are harmful to humans.

Disease can also be caused by fungi or protozoa. Fungi are organisms that have many cells. Fungi have some characteristics of plants, but they cannot be classified as plants. Molds, mushrooms, and yeasts are fungi. Diseases caused by fungi include athlete's foot and yeast infections. Protozoa are one-celled organisms. A protozoan is an animal-like organism that takes in food. Malaria,

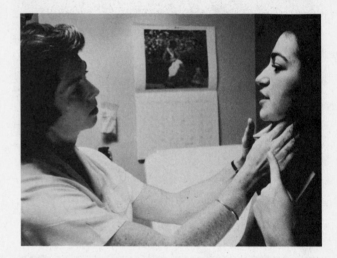

An annual checkup is good preventative medicine.

dysentery, and sleeping sickness are the diseases caused by protozoa.

Antibiotics and other drugs can be used to treat some diseases. Many viruses and bacteria can be treated with drugs or immunizations. The human body becomes immune to, or unable to have, a disease in two ways. The first way is to actually have the disease. The second way to become immune to a disease is to receive a vaccine. A **vaccine** is a solution that contains weakened or dead, disease-causing organisms. The vaccine is either injected or swallowed and produces immunity by exposing the body to this very mild, harmless form of the disease. The body then can destroy the organisms that cause the disease, and build up strength to overcome the disease in the future.

A disease that can be passed from one person to another is a **communicable disease.** Strep throat, measles, AIDS, chicken pox, and the mumps are all communicable diseases. An **epidemic** breaks out when a large number of people get the same disease in a short period of time.

How are diseases controlled and prevented? The use of public health services dates back to the eighteenth century. At that time, people began to realize that the health of a community was related to the health of each person within it. Today, public and private health agencies work to promote better public health. The aim of all health agencies is to prevent diseases, promote physical and mental health, and prolong life. ■

Lesson Review

Fill in the circle containing the letter of the term or phrase that correctly completes each statement.

1. A(n) _____ is a condition of the body that impairs the performance of the body.
   - (a) immunization
   - (b) bacterium
   - (c) virus
   - (d) disease

2. Disease can be caused by _____.
   - (a) viruses and bacteria only
   - (b) bacteria and fungi only
   - (c) fungi and protozoa only
   - (d) viruses, bacteria, fungi, and protozoa

3. _____ drugs can destroy viruses.
   - (a) All
   - (b) Many
   - (c) Some
   - (d) No

4. Tuberculosis and strep throat are diseases caused by _____.
   - (a) viruses
   - (b) bacteria
   - (c) fungi
   - (d) protozoa

5. One way to become immune to a disease is to _____.
   - (a) take antibiotics
   - (b) become allergic to it
   - (c) have the disease
   - (d) have an X ray taken

6. A(n) _____ is a solution that contains weakened or dead organisms.
   - (a) immune
   - (b) disease
   - (c) vaccine
   - (d) fungi

7. A(n) _____ occurs when a large number of people get the same disease in a short period of time.
   - (a) epidemic
   - (b) immunity
   - (c) outbreak
   - (d) vaccine

8. The aim of public and private health agencies is to _____.
   - (a) help to prevent diseases
   - (b) promote mental and physical health
   - (c) prolong life
   - (d) all of the above

● 9. Tetanus shots can kill the organisms that cause tetanus. Tetanus is caused by _____.
   - (a) epidemic
   - (b) immunizations
   - (c) bacteria
   - (d) vaccines

● 10. _____ is caused by a communicable disease.
   - (a) A bacteria
   - (b) Protozoa
   - (c) An epidemic
   - (d) All of the above

Recall that a disease is a condition of the body, or a part of the body, that impairs the performance of the body or one of its parts. **AIDS,** or acquired immune deficiency syndrome, is a communicable disease that results in the breakdown of the body's immune system. AIDS is acquired. It cannot be inherited. AIDS is a **syndrome,** a group of symptoms that occur together.

The AIDS virus does not seem to be a single isolated virus. Rather, many scientists believe that AIDS is caused by a group of related viruses commonly referred to as **HIV,** or human immunodeficiency virus. Viruses that have been removed from AIDS patients constantly change while they are being studied in the laboratory.

Some people infected with the AIDS virus develop AIDS-related complex, or **ARC,** which is a condition whose symptoms include persistent fever, diarrhea, fatigue, and swollen lymph nodes. Scientific research has shown that most people with ARC will develop AIDS.

HIV is a very fragile virus. Unlike some viruses which can be transmitted, or passed on, from person to person through the air or by touch, HIV can infect a person only by directly entering the bloodstream. Often, the infected person shows no signs or symptoms of the disease for a long time. The **incubation period,** or the time between the infection by a virus and the appearance of symptoms, of HIV can range from six months to as long as seven or more years.

How then does a person know if he or she has been infected by the AIDS virus? A blood test can be done to check for antibodies that indicate infection by the AIDS virus.

Some general symptoms of AIDS include

- unexplained, excessive tiredness.
- unexplained weight loss of ten pounds or more than ten percent of the body weight.
- long-lasting enlargement of the glands in the neck, armpits, or groin.
- long-lasting cough or sore throat.
- white patches in the mouth that do not go away.
- persistent diarrhea.
- recurring fever, chills, or night sweats.
- unexplained bleeding from any part of the body.
- reddish-purple blotches on the skin or inside the mouth, nose, eyelids, or rectum.

How is AIDS transmitted? AIDS can be transmitted from male to male, female to female, male to female, and female to male. The AIDS virus is known to be transmitted by sexual contact, by sharing blood-contaminated needles, through transfusion of infected blood or blood products, and during pregnancy from an infected mother to her unborn child.

Sexual, anal, and oral intercourse with an infected partner can transmit the AIDS virus. During sexual intercourse, the AIDS virus can enter the bloodstream of the uninfected partner from semen or from vaginal fluids. During anal intercourse, infected semen can enter the bloodstream through tears in the rectal tissue. Also, if the virus is present in the blood of the rectal tissue, it can enter the bloodstream of the uninfected partner. AIDS can also be transmitted through oral-genital intercourse.

Currently, the chance is slight that a person will be infected by AIDS from a blood transfusion in the United States. Since March 1985,

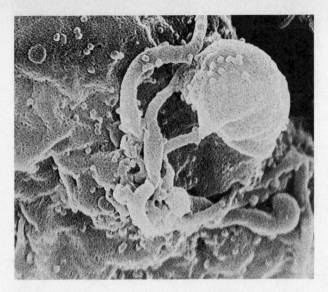

This picture, taken by an electron microscope, shows a bud of the AIDS virus on a normal cell.

all donated blood in the United States is tested for the AIDS antibodies. AIDS cannot be contracted by giving blood, because disposable needles are used to collect the blood. However, since HIV infects people when it enters the bloodstream, the sharing of blood-contaminated needles is a high risk behavior.

AIDS cannot be transmitted by handling objects touched by people with AIDS. Nor can the disease be passed on by eating food cooked or served by people with AIDS. AIDS cannot be transmitted by ordinary touching, hugging, or kissing those with AIDS. Also, people do not become infected with AIDS through the use of toilets, through mosquito bites, or through the tears cried by a person with AIDS. ■

Lesson Review

Identify each of the following statements as true or false. Correct each false statement by crossing out the word or phrase that makes it false and by writing the correct word or phrase above it.

_____ 1. AIDS results in the breakdown of the body's immune system.

_____ 2. HIV is a group of closely related viruses that causes AIDS.

_____ 3. Most people with ARC will develop AIDS.

_____ 4. Unlike some viruses that can be passed on from person to person by touch, HIV can infect a person only by entering the bloodstream.

_____ 5. Unexplained bleeding from any part of the body is not a symptom of AIDS.

_____ 6. AIDS cannot be transmitted from females to males.

_____ 7. During sexual intercourse, AIDS can be transmitted through vaginal fluids or through semen.

_____ 8. Currently, there is a very high chance that AIDS will be spread through blood transfusions in the United States.

● _____ 9. AIDS can be transmitted through closed-mouth kissing.

● _____ 10. Prostitution may spread AIDS.

Occupational therapists work with people who have physical disabilities.

Dietitians select foods for their nutritional value and plan menus that include such foods. Most dietitians work in hospitals where they consult with doctors and nurses to provide appropriate meals for recovering patients. Some dietitians plan menus for universities, colleges, and public schools. A few dietitians work for private companies with large cafeterias.

Nurses usually take charge of the routine care of patients in hospitals and medical centers. They work closely with physicians and other staff members to make sure that patients receive proper treatment. Some hospital nurses attend and assist in surgery. Nurses also work in public health programs where they take care of large numbers of people and often go into homes to provide personalized care. Some nurses are nurse practitioners who have additional and specialized training in such areas as childbirth, the care of young children, and the care of the elderly.

Obstetricians are physicians who specialize in the care of women during pregnancy, childbirth, and the six-week period following childbirth. During pregnancy, obstetricians supervise and monitor the health of both the mother and the unborn child. At childbirth, the obstetrician helps to deliver the baby safely. After childbirth, the obstetrician guides the mother's recovery. **Nurse-midwives** also provide similar services to women who will most probably have a normal delivery.

Nurse-midwives advise mothers during pregnancy, assist with the actual birth, and give care and advice during the recovery period.

Therapists of various kinds work with people to overcome problems. Occupational therapists work with people with mental and physical disabilities. They teach useful skills that help these people to lessen or overcome their disabilities. Physical therapists use exercise, heat, or ultraviolet light to treat certain ailments. Speech therapists work with people who have speech and hearing problems. Most therapists are members of the staffs of hospitals, but some are in private practices.

Public health workers perform a variety of duties for federal, state, and local governments. They provide services designed to safeguard public health. Public health workers deliver health maintenance information to families and individuals, supervise the licensing and inspection of restaurants and other food preparation establishments, and furnish support to other health workers. Almost all public health workers work for government agencies.

Numerous opportunities exist in the various fields of human health. Technical training is readily available in most communities for many positions in the field. In some areas of human health, on-the-job training opportunities exist that can lead to a position as a technician or a health-services assistant. ■

For Further Information

More information about these and related careers is available from the following publications and organizations.

Careers in Health and Fitness, Jackie Heron, Rosen Group, 1988

Careers in Health Services, Diane Seide, Lodestar, 1982

National League of Nursing
10 Columbus Circle
New York, NY 10019

American Occupational Therapy Association
1383 Piccard Drive
Rockville, MD 20850

The American Dietetic Association
430 North Michigan Avenue
Chicago, IL 60601

American Physical Therapy Association
1111 North Fairfax Street
Alexandria, VA 22314

Glossary

The boldfaced numbers after each entry indicate the page on which the word is first defined.

abdomen (p. 63)—the part of an insect's body behind the thorax that is used to digest food, remove wastes, reproduce, and breathe

acid rain (p. 28)—precipitation that forms when certain air pollutants mix with moisture in the atmosphere

acquired behavior (p. 59)—behavior that is learned

adaptation (p. 59)—a trait that helps an organism to survive in its environment

aeration (p. 25)—the process in which oxygen is restored to water

agricultural wastes (p. 28)—farm-related wastes, such as the fertilizers and pesticides used on crops, that cause pollution when they are washed into rivers by rain water as it runs off farmlands

AIDS (p. 98)—acquired immune deficiency syndrome; a communicable disease that results in the breakdown of the body's immune system

air pollution (p. 42)—the addition of harmful amounts of certain gases, chemicals, and tiny particles of solid matter to the air

air pressure (p. 34)—a force per unit area of air that pushes against Earth's surface

alveoli (p. 78)—tiny air sacs in human lungs

amphibians (p. 64)—cold-blooded vertebrates that live part of their lives in water and part on land

angiosperms (p. 52)—seed plants that produce seeds inside a fruit

antennae (p. 62)—sensory organs located between the eyes of an insect

antibiotics (p. 94)—prescription drugs used to combat bacteria

aquifer (p. 24)—a layer of rock or sediments that can transmit ground water freely

ARC (p. 98)—AIDS-related complex; a condition whose symptoms include persistent fever, diarrhea, fatigue, and swollen lymph nodes

arteries (p. 74)—blood vessels in the human body that carry blood away from the heart

artesian well (p. 24)—a well in which water rises above the level where it was first encountered

asteroids (p. 5)—fragments of matter similar to the matter that formed the planets

atmosphere (p. 32)—a mixture of solids, liquids, and gases that surrounds Earth and extends hundreds of miles above its surface

atrium (p. 74)—the right or left upper chamber of the human heart

auditory canal (p. 83)—a tube that amplifies sound waves and protects the human inner ear from dust, water, and changes in temperature

auditory nerve (p. 83)—the nerve in the human ear that forwards auditory impulses to the brain

axon (p. 80)—a branching tube that extends from a cell body and carries impulses from the cell body to the next neuron

bacteria (p. 96)—one major group of the organisms called monerans

barometer (p. 34)—an instrument that measures air pressure

beaks (p. 62)—hard, bony mouth parts of birds that are adapted to the kinds of food eaten by birds

Big Bang (p. 4)—a theory that states that the universe began about 15 billion years ago with an explosion that threw matter and energy in all directions

biology (p. 46)—the study of living things

birds (p. 62)—warm-blooded vertebrates whose bodies are covered with feathers

blizzard (p. 39)—a snowstorm that combines temperatures of 10°F and lower with winds of at least 35 miles per hour

bronchial tubes (p. 78)—small tubes in human lungs

budding (p. 58)—a form of sexual reproduction in which a small bud develops on the surface of the parent, grows, separates, and forms a new organism

Calorie (p. 92)—a measure of the energy in foods

capillaries (p. 74)—tiny blood vessels that connect veins and arteries

carbohydrate (p. 92)—an energy-rich compound made up of carbon, hydrogen, and oxygen

carnivores (p. 60)—animals that eat other animals

cartilage (p. 66)—a tough, flexible tissue

cartography (p. 14)—the science of map-making

catalytic converters (p. 42)—devices installed on automobile exhaust systems that recirculate harmful gases for more complete burning before they are released into the air

cell body (p. 80)—the part of a neuron that contains the cytoplasm, a nucleus, and other parts of the cell

cell membrane (p. 46)—a thin layer of proteins and fats that holds the different parts of a cell together

cells (p. 46)—the basic building blocks of life

cell wall (p. 46)—a rigid layer that shapes and supports a plant cell

central nervous system (p. 80)—the system composed of the brain and spinal cord that allows messages to move back and forth between the human brain and the rest of the body

chlorophyll (p. 46)—a green substance that most plants contain and use to make food

chloroplasts (p. 48)—special structures in the cells of green plants that contain chlorophyll

cholesterol (p. 92)—a fat that has been linked with heart disease and other circulatory problems

chromosomes (p. 54)—threadlike structures made of genes that carry the genetic material DNA

cilia (p. 78)—tiny hairs that line the membrane of the human nasal passages

cirrus clouds (p. 36)—thin, whispy clouds made of ice crystals

climate (p. 35)—the average weather conditions in an area over several decades

cloning (p. 55)—a process in which new plants are developed from one cell of a parent plant and have identical traits to the parent plant

clouds (p. 22)—collections of water droplets suspended in the atmosphere

cochlea (p. 83)—a structure in the human inner ear filled with fluid that vibrates when sound waves are sent from the middle ear

cold-blooded animal (p. 64)—an animal that cannot keep a constant body temperature

cold front (p. 40)—a front that develops when a cold air mass meets a warm air mass

combination foods (p. 92)—foods that include servings from the four basic food groups

comets (p. 5)—masses of frozen gases, dust, and small pieces of rock

communicable disease (p. 96)—a disease that can be passed from one person to another

condensation (p. 21)—the process by which a gas changes to a liquid

conservation (p. 25)—the wise and careful use of Earth's resources

core (p. 12)—the innermost region of Earth

cornea (p. 80)—the transparent covering that protects the front portion of the human eye and allows light to enter the eye

craters (p. 8)—bowl-shaped areas on a planet's or satellite's surface

crust (p. 12)—the outer layer of Earth

cumulus clouds (p. 36)—thick, puffy clouds made of water drops, ice, or both

cytoplasm (p. 46)—a jellylike substance that contains many cell materials, such as proteins, waste products, and dissolved minerals

dendrites (p. 80)—extensions of a cell body that receive stimuli

depressants (p. 94)—drugs that decrease the activity of the nervous system

desalination (p. 26)—a process that removes salts from seawater

dew point (p. 35)—the temperature at which condensation occurs

diaphragm (p. 78)—a strong sheet of muscles located beneath human lungs

digestive tract (p. 76)—a long tube in the human body through which food passes

disease (p. 96)—a condition of the body or one of its parts that impairs the performance of the body or the body part

dominant trait (p. 54)—a trait that shows up and prevents another form of the trait from being seen

drug (p. 94)—any substance, other than food, which can change life processes within the body

eardrum (p. 83)—a thin sheet of tissue at the end of the auditory canal that separates the human outer ear from the middle ear

endangered species (p. 69)—a species that must be protected so that it does not become extinct

endoplasmic reticulum or ER (p. 72)—the transportation network of a cell formed by small, tubelike structures housed in the cytoplasm

enzyme (p. 76)—a substance that speeds up the rate of a chemical reaction

epidemic (p. 96)—a condition that occurs when a large number of people get the same disease in a short period of time

equator (p. 10)—an imaginary line that separates Earth into the Northern and Southern Hemispheres

esophagus (p. 76)—a tube in the human body that connects the mouth with the stomach

eustachian tube (p. 83)—a tube connecting the human middle ear with the throat

evaporation (p. 21)—the process by which a liquid changes to a gas

exoskeleton (p. 62)—the hard, external skeleton of an insect

exosphere (p. 33)—the upper section of the thermosphere

external fertilization (p. 59)—sexual reproduction in which the sperm joins the egg outside the female's body

extinction (p. 59)—the total disappearance of a species

fault (p. 13)—a large fracture along which movement has taken place

fertilization (p. 53)—the joining of the male and female sex cells to produce a zygote

filtration (p. 25)—the removal of suspended materials in water through the use of filters

fins (p. 66)—bony structures covered with webs of skin that aid a fish in swimming

fish (p. 66)—cold-blooded vertebrates that live in fresh or salt water and that obtain oxygen from the water through gills

fossils (p. 12)—the remains of animals and plants preserved in Earth's crust

frequency (p. 82)—the number of waves that pass a given point in one second

fronts (p. 40)—boundaries between air masses having different properties

galaxy (p. 4)—a large grouping of billions of stars, dust, and gas

gas (p. 20)—the state of matter that has no fixed volume or shape

genes (p. 54)—cell structures that control the inheritance of traits from parents to offspring

genetics (p. 54)—the scientific study of heredity

geology (p. 12)—the study of planet Earth and the processes that change it

germination (p. 53)—the early growth of a plant from a seed

gills (p. 64)—small slits located behind the heads of water animals that allow them to breathe

glaciers (p. 21)—masses of ice in motion

gravity (p. 8)—the attraction between two objects due to their masses

ground water (p. 24)—precipitation that soaks into the ground after reaching Earth's surface

gymnosperms (p. 52)—seed plants whose seeds are not protected by being formed inside a fruit

habitat (p. 47)—a place in which a living thing naturally lives

hail (p. 36)—small balls or chunks of ice that fall from cumulonimbus clouds

hallucinogens (p. 95)—drugs that cause users to imagine sights and sounds that do not exist

heart (p. 74)—a strong, muscular, four-chambered pump that powers the human body's circulatory system

herbivores (p. 60)—animals that eat plants

heredity (p. 54)—the passing of certain characteristics, or traits, from parents to offspring

HIV (p. 98)—human immunodeficiency virus; a group of related viruses that many scientists believe might cause AIDS

humidity (p. 35)—moisture in the atmosphere

hurricane (p. 39)—a tropical storm that forms over an ocean

hybrid form (p. 54)—the form of a trait that results when dominant and recessive genes combine

hydrocarbons (p. 42)—chemical compounds that contain hydrogen and carbon

icebergs (p. 27)—large pieces of ice that break off a glacier and float in the sea

igneous rocks (p. 12)—rocks that form when hot, molten material cools and hardens

immunized (p. 91)—protected against certain diseases

inborn behavior (p. 59)—behavior that is inherited from the parents

incineration (p. 16)—the disposal of solid wastes by burning

incubation period (p. 98)—the time between infection by a virus and the onset of symptoms of a disease

industrial wastes (p. 28)—chemicals and other substances discarded during or after the manufacturing process

insects (p. 62)—small, complex invertebrates with jointed legs, segmented bodies, and a hard, external skeleton

internal fertilization (p. 59)—sexual reproduction in which the sperm and egg join inside the female's body

invertebrate (p. 58)—an animal without a backbone

ionosphere (p. 33)—the lower section of the thermosphere

ions (p. 22)—atoms with electrical charges

iris (p. 80)—the colored part of the human eye that surrounds the pupil

isobars (p. 40)—lines on a weather map that connect points that have the same barometric pressure

Jupiter (p. 6)—the fifth planet from the sun

labor (p. 85)—the beginning of childbirth during which the muscles of the uterus contract involuntarily to help push a baby out of the mother's body

land breeze (p. 39)—breeze caused when cool air over a landmass flows toward a large body of water, forcing the warm air over the water to rise

large intestine (p. 77)—an organ in the human body that removes excess water from undigested food

larynx (p. 78)—the human voice box, which is made of cartilage and contains the vocal cords

lens (p. 80)—the part of the human eye that focuses light rays and transmits them to the back surface of the eye

lines of latitude (p. 14)—(See parallels.)

lines of longitude (p. 14)—(See meridians.)

liquid (p. 20)—the state of matter that has a constant volume, but no fixed shape

low pressure system (p. 40)—an area of low pressure that forms between a warm front and a cold front

mammals (p. 60)—vertebrates that have hair on their bodies and produce milk to feed their young

mantle (p. 12)—the middle layer of Earth that surrounds the core

Mars (p. 6)—the fourth planet from the sun

matter (p. 20)—anything that has mass and takes up space

melting (p. 21)—the process by which a solid changes to a liquid

menstrual cycle (p. 84)—the human female reproductive cycle that averages 28 days and involves the maturation of the egg in the ovary

menstruation (p. 84)—a process during which blood and other tissues are shed from the human uterus through the vagina

Mercury (p. 6)—the closest planet to the sun

meridians (p. 14)—imaginary lines running north and south on a globe or map; also called lines of longitude

mesosphere (p. 33)—the layer of air about 30–50 miles above Earth's surface

metamorphic rocks (p. 12)—rocks that are changed by intense heat and pressure

metamorphosis (p. 63)—the series of growth changes in some animals

meteorites (p. 5)—meteoroids that reach Earth's surface without burning up

meteoroids (p. 5)—small chunks of iron and rock, probably formed from collisions among asteroids

meteorology (p. 40)—the science of forecasting the weather

meteors (p. 5)—streaks of light given off by meteoroids that burn up in Earth's atmosphere

Milky Way (p. 4)—the galaxy that includes Earth

minerals (p. 92)—elements found in nature that are needed by the human body in small amounts

mitochondria (p. 73)—rod-shaped structures in a cell's cytoplasm that release energy for use in the cell

molting (p. 64)—the process in which some animals shed their skins

mountains (p. 10)—any land area that rises sharply above the surrounding area

narcotics (p. 95)—depressants that relieve pain and often cause drowsiness

Neptune (p. 7)—the eighth planet from the sun

neuron (p. 80)—the nerve cell that is the basic structure of the human nervous system

nitrogen (p. 32)—the most abundant gas in Earth's atmosphere

nonvascular (p. 50)—without tissues for carrying food and water through the plant

nucleus (p. 54)—the part of a cell that contains the genetic material deoxyribonucleic acid (DNA)

nutrients (p. 90)—substances needed by the body for various life activities

nutrition (p. 90)—the study of food and its use by the human body

occluded front (p. 40)—a front that forms when two air masses join and force the warmer air between them aloft

omnivores (p. 60)—animals that eat both plants and other animals

orbit (p. 6)—the circular path a planet takes around the sun

organ (p. 73)—a group of tissues that work together to perform one or more life activities

ovaries (p. 84)—the human female reproductive organs that produce eggs

ovulation (p. 84)—the process of releasing a female egg from an ovary into an oviduct, or fallopian tube

ovule (p. 53)—the female part of a flower that contains the egg

oxygen (p. 32)—a gas that makes up about 21 percent of Earth's air

ozone (p. 33)—a form of oxygen that absorbs most of the dangerous ultraviolet rays of the sun

parallels (p. 14)—imaginary lines running east and west on a globe or map; also called lines of latitude

peripheral nervous system (p. 80)—the system made up of all of the nerves in the human body that are not part of the central nervous system

peristalsis (p. 76)—the reflex muscle motion that causes food to move from the esophagus to the stomach and on through the rest of the human digestive system

physical addiction (p. 94)—a condition in which a drug user must continue to take a drug in order to avoid withdrawal symptoms

photosynthesis (p. 48)—the process by which the leaves of green plants use light energy to produce food

pistils (p. 52)—female plant structures that produce egg cells

plains (p. 10)—large, flat, low-lying areas of land

plaque (p. 91)—a sticky material that forms on teeth within 20 minutes after eating

plasma (p. 74)—a clear, watery fluid that makes up about 55 percent of the total volume of human blood

plate tectonics (p. 13)—a theory that states that Earth's crust and upper mantle can be divided into large sections called plates

plateaus (p. 10)—high, relatively flat areas of land

platelets (p. 75)—tiny, colorless structures in human blood that help it to clot

Pluto (p. 7)—the planet that is usually the most distant from the sun

poaching (p. 68)—the illegal hunting of animals

polar easterlies (p. 38)—winds that blow between the poles and 60° north and south latitudes

polar zones (p. 35)—the areas that extend from each pole to $66\frac{1}{2}°$ north and south latitudes

pollination (p. 52)—the carrying of pollen grains by wind, water, and animals to the pistils of a flower

population explosion (p. 26)—the rapid increase in the number of humans living on Earth at one time

precipitation (p. 22)—moisture released by clouds, such as rain, snow, sleet, or hail

prevailing westerlies (p. 38)—the major wind system between 30° north and 60° north latitudes and 30° south and 60° south latitudes

prey (p. 65)—an animal that is eaten by another animal

prime meridian (p. 14)—an imaginary line designated 0° longitude

psychological addiction (p. 94)—the condition in which a drug user has developed an emotional need for a drug

puberty (p. 84)—the time when human beings are first able to reproduce

pupil (p. 80)—the opening in the human eye beneath the cornea

rare species (p. 68)—a species that has very few living members

recessive trait (p. 54)—a trait that is masked or hidden when the dominant form of the trait appears

recycle (p. 16)—to reuse natural resources; to make solid wastes ready for using again

red blood cells (p. 74)—cells in human blood plasma that carry oxygen and make up about 44 percent of blood's volume

regeneration (p. 58)—a form of asexual reproduction in which lost body parts are regrown, or regenerated

reptiles (p. 64)—cold-blooded vertebrates with dry, scaly skins that prevent water loss

reservoir (p. 25)—an artificial lake to store fresh water

respiration (p. 48)—the process by which oxygen is combined with food and energy is released

retina (p. 80)—the back surface of the human eye that is attached to the optic nerve

revolve (p. 8)—to circle, such as the path followed by Earth around the sun

ribosomes (p. 73)—small, circular structures in a cell that make proteins

ridge of high pressure (p. 41)—a belt of air that brings sunny skies and pleasant weather

rotation (p. 8)—the spinning about an axis

satellite (p. 8)—an object that revolves, or spins, around a larger, primary object

Saturn (p. 7)—the sixth planet from the sun

scrotum (p. 84)—the sac that encloses the human male testes

sea breeze (p. 39)—a breeze that forms when cool air over a large body of water flows inland and causes the warm air over the land to rise

sea level (p. 10)—zero feet elevation

sedimentary rocks (p. 12)—rocks that form when pieces of Earth's material become cemented together by natural processes

sediments (p. 24)—unconsolidated particles of Earth's crust such as mud, clay, sand, gravel, and pebbles

semen (p. 85)—a whitish fluid containing sperm

sepals (p. 52)—the tough, leaflike, green coverings that protect the young flower from cold and other injuries

sewage (p. 28)—liquid and solid waste carried by sewers or drains

skin (p. 91)—a body organ that regulates temperature and provides a barrier against certain diseases

sleet (p. 36)—precipitation that freezes after it leaves a cloud and before it reaches the ground

small intestine (p. 76)—a coiled tube in the human body in which most chemical digestion takes place

smog (p. 42)—a combination of smoke, certain gases, and fog

solar system (p. 5)—the part of the Milky Way that includes the sun and all the natural objects that travel around it

solid (p. 20)—the state of matter that has both a definite shape and a definite volume

solid wastes (p. 16)—items discarded after use, including paper, plastic, glass and metal containers, garbage, packing and packaging materials, and junked automobiles

solidification (p. 21)—the process by which a liquid changes to a solid

sound (p. 82)—a rhythmic disturbance of air that carries energy

species (p. 47)—a subgroup of organisms in a kingdom whose members are able to reproduce

spores (p. 50)—reproductive cells produced by some nonvascular plants

stamens (p. 52)—male plant structures that produce pollen grains

stationary fronts (p. 40)—fronts that develop when either a warm or a cold front stops advancing

stimulants (p. 94)—drugs that increase the rate of the body's nervous system

stomata (p. 48)—small openings in the leaves of plants through which oxygen, carbon dioxide, and water vapor enter and exit

stratosphere (p. 32)—the layer of air that begins about ten miles above Earth's surface and extends upward to about 30 miles

stratus clouds (p. 36)—dull gray clouds nearest Earth's surface

syndrome (p. 98)—a group of symptoms of a disease that occur together

system (p. 73)—a group of organs that work together to carry on life activities

temperate zones (p. 35)—areas located between the polar zones and the tropics

temperature (p. 34)—a measure of the hotness or coldness of a body, or the amount of internal energy it contains

testes (p. 84)—the two oval-shaped glands of the human male reproductive organs in which sperm are produced

thermosphere (p. 33)—the outermost layer of Earth's atmosphere

thorax (p. 63)—the upper part of an insect's body to which the legs and wings are attached

threatened species (p. 68)—a species that may be common in some areas but its members are generally decreasing in numbers

thunderstorms (p. 39)—severe storms that form when masses of warm air rapidly invade masses of cool air

tissues (p. 73)—groups of similar cells that work together to perform a special job

tornado (p. 39)—a funnel-shaped wind storm that moves in a narrow path over land

trachea (p. 78)—the tube that carries air to a human's lungs

trade winds (p. 38)—winds that flow between the equator and the tropics

transfer station (p. 16)—a place where solid wastes are stored temporarily

transpiration (p. 48)—the loss of water vapor through the stomata of a leaf

tropical zone (p. 35)—the area between $23\frac{1}{2}^{\circ}$ north and south latitudes

troposphere (p. 32)—the layer of air nearest Earth's surface

universe (p. 4)—all matter and energy and the space that they occupy

Uranus (p. 7)—the seventh planet from the sun

uterus (p. 84)—a hollow organ in a human female that is about the size of a pear and that has a narrow opening that leads to the vagina

vaccine (p. 96)—a solution containing weakened or dead organisms that is injected or swallowed to produce immunity by exposing the body to a very mild, harmless form of a disease

vagina (p. 84)—a body canal that leads to the outside of a human female's body

vascular plant (p. 50)—a plant that has tissues for moving essential nutrients through the plant

veins (p. 74)—blood vessels that carry blood to the heart

ventricles (p. 74)—the right or left lower chambers of the human heart

Venus (p. 6)—the second planet from the sun

vertebrate (p. 58)—an animal with a backbone

villi (p. 77)—small, fingerlike projections that cover the lining of a human's small intestine

virus (p. 96)—a compound that has characteristics of both living and nonliving things

vitamins (p. 92)—organic compounds used by the body to regulate changes in the cells

warm-blooded animal (p. 60)—an animal that has an almost constant body temperature

warm fronts (p. 40)—fronts that develop when a warm air mass meets a cold air mass

water cycle (p. 21)—the exchange of water among Earth's land, water bodies, and atmosphere

water pollution (p. 28)—the introduction of chemicals and wastes into bodies of water that make the water unhealthful

water table (p. 24)—the upper limit of the zone of saturation; the highest space occupied by ground water

weather (p. 34)—the state or condition of the atmosphere at any given time and place

weather map (p. 40)—the outline map of an area for which a forecast will be made

white blood cells (p. 75)—cells produced in bone marrow, lymph nodes, and the spleen that protect the body against infection

wildlife preservation (p. 68)—the maintaining of a species in order to protect it from becoming extinct

wind (p. 35)—air in motion

zoology (p. 58)—the branch of biology that focuses mainly on the study of animals

zooplankton (p. 67)—small, drifting, or weakly swimming animals at or near the surface of many bodies of water

zygote (p. 50)—a fertilized female egg cell

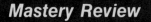

Mastery Review

This Mastery Review is an opportunity to check your understanding of the content of this book. Part 1 measures the first four units, and Part 2 measures the last three units.

This Mastery Review should take no longer than one hour to complete. If you come to questions that you cannot answer, move on. When you have answered the questions that you know, try those that you skipped. To record your answers, fill in the numbered space on your answer sheet that matches the number of the correct answer.

Part 1 (Sections A, B, and C cover material in Units 1–4.)

A. In questions 1–17, a phrase is followed by four terms. Mark the term that the phrase best defines or identifies.

1. a large fracture in Earth's crust along which movement has taken place
   (1) plate   (2) fault   (3) mantle   (4) solid waste

2. the line that separates Earth into the Northern and Southern Hemispheres
   (1) warm front   (2) date line   (3) equator   (4) ion

3. the upper limit of the zone of saturation
   (1) fault   (2) water table   (3) plains   (4) habitat

4. the process by which a gas changes to a liquid
   (1) melting   (2) evaporation   (3) humidity   (4) condensation

5. clouds nearest Earth's surface
   (1) stratus   (2) plateaus   (3) cumulus   (4) temperature

6. the process by which leaves of green plants use light energy to produce food
   (1) gravity   (2) evaporation   (3) photosynthesis (4) cytoplasm

7. the early growth of a plant from a seed
   (1) fertilization (2) pollination   (3) nourishment   (4) germination

8. a large grouping of billions of stars, dust, and gas
   (1) solar system   (2) asteroid   (3) universe   (4) galaxy

9. millions of water droplets suspended in the atmosphere
   (1) precipitation (2) clouds   (3) ions   (4) glaciers

10. a place in which an organism naturally lives
    (1) preserve   (2) habitat   (3) stomata   (4) cell

113

11. control the inheritance of traits from parents to offspring

    (1) ERs   (2) cells   (3) genes   (4) capillaries

12. has a constant volume but no fixed shape

    (1) liquid   (2) gas   (3) solid   (4) all of the above

13. a layer of rock or sediments that transmits ground water freely

    (1) climate   (2) glacier   (3) reservoir   (4) aquifer

14. moisture in the atmosphere

    (1) dew point   (2) humidity   (3) temperature   (4) climate

15. the largest planet

    (1) Jupiter   (2) Neptune   (3) Saturn   (4) Pluto

16. high, relatively flat, uplifted land areas

    (1) glaciers   (2) mountains   (3) plateaus   (4) plains

17. Earth's middle layer

    (1) core   (2) mantle   (3) crust   (4) plate

B. Questions 18–31 each contain a blank space and are followed by four choices. Mark the word or phrase that best completes each statement.

18. Roughly 78 percent of Earth's air is _____.

    (1) ozone   (2) nitrogen   (3) oxygen   (4) water

19. _____ is anything that has mass and takes up space.

    (1) Matter   (2) Gravity   (3) Geology   (4) Genetics

20. Almost _____ percent of Earth's surface is water.

    (1) 20   (2) 75   (3) 95   (4) 40

21. Tides are caused by the pull of _____ among Earth, the moon, and the sun.

    (1) rotation   (2) gravity   (3) revolution   (4) nitrogen

22. Earth's orbit around the sun is _____.

    (1) circular   (2) rectangular   (3) oval-shaped   (4) tilted

23. _____ is a jellylike substance inside a cell that contains many cell materials, such as proteins, waste products, and dissolved minerals.

    (1) Chlorophyll (2) Sediment   (3) Precipitation (4) Cytoplasm

24. When air can't hold the water vapor that it contains, the water vapor _____.

    (1) falls   (2) evaporates   (3) rises   (4) increases

25. Fossils are commonly found in _____ rocks.

    (1) metamorphic (2) sedimentary   (3) moon   (4) rounded

26. Day and night are caused by Earth's _____.
    (1) precipitation   (2) tides   (3) rotation   (4) size

27. Plate tectonics is a theory stating that Earth can be divided into large sections called _____.
    (1) plates   (2) faults   (3) continents   (4) zones

28. _____ are small chunks of iron and rock that travel through space.
    (1) Asterisks   (2) Comets   (3) Moons   (4) Meteoroids

29. Loose particles, such as mud, clay, sand, gravel, and pebbles, are called _____.
    (1) faults   (2) water tables   (3) sediments   (4) artesian wells

30. _____ removes suspended materials from water.
    (1) Evaporation   (2) Filtration   (3) Distillation   (4) Conservation

31. A _____ is a funnel-shaped wind storm that moves in a narrow path over land.
    (1) hurricane   (2) blizzard   (3) thunderstorm   (4) tornado

C. In each pair of statements in questions 32–39, one is true and the other is false. Mark the statement that is true.

32. (1) Scientists believe that Earth is the center of the universe.
    (2) Scientists know that Earth is only a tiny speck in the universe.

33. (1) Observers from Earth see only one side of the moon.
    (2) Observers from Earth see both sides of the moon.

34. (1) Algae and mosses are vascular plants.
    (2) Ferns and trees are vascular plants.

35. (1) Aeration restores the oxygen content of water.
    (2) Filtration restores the oxygen content of water.

36. (1) The distance between lines of latitude and longitude are not exactly the same at every point on a globe.
    (2) The distance between lines of latitude and longitude are exactly the same at every point on a globe.

37. (1) Plants use chlorophyll to make food.
    (2) Plants use condensation to make food.

38. (1) The equator is 90° latitude.
    (2) The equator is 0° latitude.

39. (1) Climate is the average of all weather conditions in an area over several decades.
    (2) Climate is the state or condition of the atmosphere at any given time and place.

Part 2 (Sections D, E, and F are based on material in Units 5–7.)

D. In questions 40–52, a phrase is followed by four terms. Mark the term that the phrase best defines or identifies.

40. the study of living things
    (1) geology   (2) cartography   (3) periostalsis   (4) biology

41. animals that live part of their lives on water and part on land
    (1) insects   (2) amphibians   (3) reptiles   (4) mammals

42. valuable food for many sea animals
    (1) cartilage   (2) molting   (3) poaching   (4) zooplankton

43. groups of similar cells that work together to perform a similar job
    (1) vitamins   (2) tissues   (3) systems   (4) chromosomes

44. the basic structure of the human nervous system
    (1) neuron   (2) ion   (3) cornea   (4) vitamins

45. the egg-producing organs in the human female
    (1) vagina   (2) cochlea   (3) auditory canals   (4) ovaries

46. a fat that has been linked with heart disease
    (1) protein   (2) cholesterol   (3) Calorie   (4) carbohydrate

47. drugs that increase the rate of the body's nervous system
    (1) stimulants   (2) depressants   (3) narcotics   (4) hallucinogens

48. a trait that helps an organism survive
    (1) habitat   (2) adaptation   (3) gene   (4) extinction

49. animals that eat only other animals
    (1) endangered   (2) herbivores   (3) arboreals   (4) carnivores

50. used by an insect to feel, smell, taste, and hear
    (1) zygote   (2) thorax   (3) exoskeleton   (4) antennae

51. the process by which snakes shed their skin
    (1) poaching   (2) metamorphosis   (3) molting   (4) respiration

52. a species that must be protected in order to survive
    (1) extinct   (2) omnivore   (3) endangered   (4) reptile

E. Questions 53–66, each contain a blank space and are followed by four choices. Mark the word or phrase that best completes each statement.

53. The _____ is the tube that carries air to the human lungs.

    (1) cilia   (2) vagina   (3) diaphragm   (4) trachea

54. As part of their health program, children are _____ to protect them against certain diseases.

    (1) immunized   (2) sterilized   (3) addicted   (4) systematized

55. A group of tissues that work together to perform one or more of life's activities is a(n) _____.

    (1) artery   (2) system   (3) organ   (4) vein

56. _____ carry the blood away from the human heart.

    (1) Arteries   (2) Ventricles   (3) Red blood cells   (4) Capillaries

57. Tiny structures in blood that help it clot are called _____.

    (1) plasma   (2) platelets   (3) red cells   (4) nutrients

58. A _____ is a measure of the energy in foods.

    (1) mineral   (2) Calorie   (3) carbohydrate   (4) protein

59. _____ are prescription drugs used to combat bacteria.

    (1) Antibiotics   (2) Tranquilizers   (3) Narcotics   (4) Stimulants

60. Light enters the human eye through the _____.

    (1) cochlea   (2) iris   (3) auditory canal   (4) cornea

61. _____ carries food and oxygen to body tissues.

    (1) Water   (2) Nitrogen   (3) Blood   (4) ER

62. The _____ connects the middle ear with the throat.

    (1) cornea   (2) eardrum   (3) cochlea   (4) eustachian tube

63. Fish get oxygen from water through their _____.

    (1) gills   (2) fins   (3) cartilage   (4) tails

64. _____ do not have internal skeletons.

    (1) Mammals   (2) Vertebrates   (3) Amphibians   (4) Invertebrates

65. The lungs are part of the human _____ system.

    (1) circulatory   (2) reproductive   (3) respiratory   (4) digestive

66. _____ are drugs that cause users to imagine nonexistent sights and sounds.

    (1) Hallucinogens   (2) Depressants   (3) Stimulants   (4) Narcotics

F. In each pair of statements in questions 67–70, one is true and the other is false. Mark the statement that is true.

67. (1) AIDS can be transmitted by handling objects touched by people who have the disease.

    (2) AIDS cannot be transmitted by handling objects touched by people who have the disease.

68. (1) Carbon dioxide is released from the body through the cells.

    (2) Carbon dioxide is released from the body through exhalation by the lungs.

69. (1) Menstruation is the time when a human being is first able to reproduce.

    (2) Puberty is the time when a human being is first able to reproduce.

70. (1) In bright light, the iris of the eye gets larger and the pupil becomes smaller.

    (2) In bright light, the iris of the eye gets smaller and the pupil becomes larger.

Name _____

Mastery Review Answer Sheet

TEST ANSWERS

Fill in the circle corresponding to your answer for each question. Erase cleanly.

Part 1

A

1 ① ② ③ ④
2 ① ② ③ ④
3 ① ② ③ ④
4 ① ② ③ ④
5 ① ② ③ ④
6 ① ② ③ ④
7 ① ② ③ ④
8 ① ② ③ ④
9 ① ② ③ ④
10 ① ② ③ ④
11 ① ② ③ ④
12 ① ② ③ ④
13 ① ② ③ ④
14 ① ② ③ ④
15 ① ② ③ ④
16 ① ② ③ ④
17 ① ② ③ ④

B

18 ① ② ③ ④
19 ① ② ③ ④
20 ① ② ③ ④
21 ① ② ③ ④
22 ① ② ③ ④
23 ① ② ③ ④
24 ① ② ③ ④
25 ① ② ③ ④
26 ① ② ③ ④
27 ① ② ③ ④
28 ① ② ③ ④
29 ① ② ③ ④
30 ① ② ③ ④
31 ① ② ③ ④

C

32 ① ② ③ ④
33 ① ② ③ ④
34 ① ② ③ ④
35 ① ② ③ ④
36 ① ② ③ ④
37 ① ② ③ ④
38 ① ② ③ ④
39 ① ② ③ ④

Part 2

D

40 ① ② ③ ④
41 ① ② ③ ④
42 ① ② ③ ④
43 ① ② ③ ④
44 ① ② ③ ④
45 ① ② ③ ④
46 ① ② ③ ④
47 ① ② ③ ④
48 ① ② ③ ④
49 ① ② ③ ④
50 ① ② ③ ④
51 ① ② ③ ④
52 ① ② ③ ④

E

53 ① ② ③ ④
54 ① ② ③ ④
55 ① ② ③ ④
56 ① ② ③ ④
57 ① ② ③ ④
58 ① ② ③ ④
59 ① ② ③ ④
60 ① ② ③ ④
61 ① ② ③ ④
62 ① ② ③ ④
63 ① ② ③ ④
64 ① ② ③ ④
65 ① ② ③ ④
66 ① ② ③ ④

F

67 ① ② ③ ④
68 ① ② ③ ④
69 ① ② ③ ④
70 ① ② ③ ④

Answer Key

Unit 1

Lesson 1
1. d
2. f
3. a
4. h
5. c
6. b
7. g
8. e
9. j
10. i

Lesson 2
1. d
2. b
3. d
4. d
5. b
6. d
7. a
8. c
9. b
10. c

Lesson 3
1. b
2. d
3. b
4. a
5. c
6. c
7. d
8. c
9. b
10. a

Lesson 4
1. 4.5 billion
2. Mt. Everest
3. a sphere that is slightly flattened at its poles
4. three fourths
5. Plains
6. rotates
7. January
8. the angle at which the sun's rays strike a certain location
9. summer
10. 65,000

Lesson 5
1. b
2. d
3. b
4. a
5. b
6. d
7. c
8. b
9. d
10. c

Lesson 6
1. a
2. c
3. h
4. e
5. i
6. g
7. d
8. f
9. j
10. b

Issues in Science
1. d
2. d
3. a
4. d
5. b
6. a
7. c
8. d
9. c
10. c

Unit 2

Lesson 1
1. T
2. F (*mass* for *weight*)
3. T
4. F (*solid* for *gas*)
5. T
6. T
7. F (*32°* for *100°*)
8. T
9. F (*expansion* for *contraction*)
10. F (*condensation* for *melting*)

Lesson 2
1. c
2. d
3. a
4. b
5. d
6. b
7. a
8. d
9. d
10. d

Lesson 3
1. water table
2. Ground water
3. sediments
4. air
5. conservation
6. Chlorine
7. aeration
8. Filtration
9. less
10. aquifer

Lesson 4
1. F (*doubled* for *tripled*)
2. T
3. F (*Ground water provides* for *Icebergs provide*)
4. T
5. F (*harmful* for *valuable*)
6. F (*removal* for *addition*)
7. F (*fairly expensive* for *very cheap*)
8. T
9. F (*8 billion* for *100 million*)
10. F (*forty* for *four*)

Issues in Science
1. j
2. g
3. f
4. d
5. a
6. i
7. h
8. b
9. c
10. e

Unit 3

Lesson 1
1. d
2. a
3. c
4. c
5. b
6. a
7. c
8. c
9. a
10. a

Lesson 2
1. i
2. h
3. g
4. b
5. a
6. j
7. d
8. c
9. f
10. e

Lesson 3
1. d
2. b
3. b
4. b
5. a
6. d
7. c
8. c
9. b
10. c

Lesson 4
1. F *(Anemometers* for *Weather vanes)*
2. T
3. F *(equator* for *poles)*
4. T
5. F *(body of water* for *landmass)*
6. F *(an ocean* for *land)*
7. T
8. T
9. T
10. T

Lesson 5
1. b
2. c
3. a
4. d
5. b
6. a
7. a
8. d
9. a
10. d

Issues in Science
1. T
2. F *(human activities* for *natural causes)*
3. T
4. T
5. T
6. F *(screens* for *doesn't screen)*
7. T
8. F *(no longer* for *still)*
9. F *(less* for *more)*
10. T

Unit 4

Lesson 1
1. c
2. c
3. b
4. a
5. b
6. c
7. d
8. c
9. b
10. c

Lesson 2
1. F *(Leaves* for *Roots)*
2. T
3. F *(Photosynthesis* for *Transpiration)*
4. T
5. T
6. F *(stomata* for *chloroplasts)*
7. F *(transpiration* for *respiration)*
8. T
9. F *(day* for *night)*
10. T

Lesson 3
1. d
2. d
3. b
4. a
5. c
6. c
7. c
8. a
9. b
10. c

Lesson 4
1. h
2. d
3. f
4. e
5. a
6. i
7. g
8. c
9. j
10. b

Issues in Science
1. heredity
2. Gregor Mendel
3. self
4. dominant
5. nucleus
6. Genes
7. hybrid
8. Genetic engineering
9. red
10. dominant

Unit 5

Lesson 1
1. zoology
2. vertebrate
3. internal skeletons
4. invertebrate
5. asexual
6. external
7. Internal
8. Acquired
9. adapt
10. inborn

Lesson 2
1. f
2. a
3. c
4. d
5. e
6. h
7. g
8. j
9. i
10. b

Lesson 3
1. d
2. d
3. d
4. a
5. d
6. a
7. b
8. b
9. c
10. b

Lesson 4
1. Amphibians
2. cold-blooded
3. gills
4. tadpole
5. Reptiles
6. ear
7. molting
8. Water
9. prey
10. reptiles

Lesson 5
1. jawless, bony, cartilage
2. Jawless
3. fins
4. gills
5. two-chambered
6. contraction
7. Zooplankton
8. Filter feeding
9. colder
10. cartilage

Issues in Science
1. F *(it was hunted for there was too much food)*
2. T
3. F *(endangered for extinct)*
4. T
5. T
6. F *(reduced for increased)*
7. T
8. F *(an important for no)*
9. F *(less for more)*
10. F *(do become for do not become)*

Unit 6

Lesson 1
1. b
2. d
3. c
4. d
5. a
6. b
7. c
8. a
9. c
10. a

Lesson 2
1. d
2. b
3. a
4. a
5. a
6. b
7. c
8. a
9. d
10. b

Lesson 3
1. c
2. d
3. e
4. h
5. i
6. a
7. b
8. j
9. g
10. f

Lesson 4
1. nose
2. Cilia
3. movements of the tongue and mouth
4. trachea
5. alveoli
6. pleura
7. flattens
8. forced out
9. decreases
10. diaphragm

Unit 6 cont'd

Lesson 5

1. F *(central for peripheral)*
2. T
3. F *(Axons for Dendrites)*
4. T
5. F *(not involved for involved)*
6. T
7. F *(iris for lens)*
8. T
9. T
10. F *(voluntary for involuntary)*

Lesson 6

1. j
2. e
3. g
4. a
5. f
6. c
7. d
8. b
9. i
10. h

Lesson 7

1. b
2. d
3. a
4. a
5. c
6. d
7. b
8. c
9. c
10. b

Issues in Science

1. F *(low for high)*
2. F *(kidney for heart)*
3. T
4. T
5. F *(pacemaker for dialysis machine)*
6. F *(Many for Few)*
7. F *(have not produced for have produced)*
8. F *(is not able for is able)*
9. T
10. T

Unit 7

Lesson 1

1. e
2. d
3. j
4. c
5. a
6. f
7. h
8. g
9. i
10. b

Lesson 2

1. c
2. a
3. d
4. a
5. d
6. d
7. c
8. a
9. b
10. b

Lesson 3

1. drug
2. over-the-counter
3. side effect
4. Psychological
5. tranquilizers
6. depressant
7. narcotic or depressant
8. hallucinogens
9. stimulant
10. stimulants

Lesson 4

1. d
2. d
3. d
4. b
5. c
6. c
7. a
8. d
9. c
10. c

Issues in Science

1. T
2. T
3. T
4. T
5. F *(is a for is not a)*
6. F *(can for cannot)*
7. T
8. F *(low for high)*
9. F *(cannot for can)*
10. T

Mastery Review
Answer Key

Part 1

A	B	C
1. 2	18. 2	32. 2
2. 3	19. 1	33. 1
3. 2	20. 2	34. 2
4. 4	21. 2	35. 1
5. 1	22. 3	36. 1
6. 3	23. 4	37. 1
7. 4	24. 1	38. 2
8. 4	25. 2	39. 1
9. 2	26. 3	
10. 2	27. 1	
11. 3	28. 4	
12. 1	29. 3	
13. 4	30. 2	
14. 2	31. 4	
15. 1		
16. 3		
17. 2		

Part 2

D	E	F
40. 4	53. 4	67. 2
41. 2	54. 1	68. 2
42. 4	55. 3	69. 2
43. 2	56. 1	70. 1
44. 1	57. 2	
45. 4	58. 2	
46. 2	59. 1	
47. 1	60. 4	
48. 2	61. 3	
49. 4	62. 4	
50. 4	63. 1	
51. 3	64. 4	
52. 3	65. 3	
	66. 1	

Acknowledgments

Cover & inside illustrations: Robert Priest

p. 4 Harvard College Observatory; **p. 18** © Phyllis Grayber-Jenson/Stock, Boston; **p. 20** Elizabeth Willis; **p. 24** Bureau of Reclamation, U.S. Department of the Interior; **p. 28** Environmental Protection Agency; **p. 30** © George Bellerose/Stock, Boston; **p. 32** City of Miami News Bureau; **p. 34** National Weather Service; **p. 36** (both) NOAA; **p. 43** Norton; **p. 44** © David Aronson/Stock, Boston; **p. 46** C.V. Rice; **p. 50** © Eric Neurath/Stock, Boston; **p. 56** © Peter Menzel/Stock, Boston; **p. 58** Florida Department of Commerce, Division of Tourism; **p. 60** Texas Parks & Wildlife; **p.65** U.S. Fish & Wildlife Service; **p. 66** © Photo Researchers **p. 69** Smithsonian Institution; **p. 70** © Christopher Morrow/Stock, Boston; **p. 72** Tim Morse; **p. 86** University of Wisconsin; **p. 88** © John Lei/Stock, Boston; **p. 90** © Arthur Grace/Stock, Boston; **p. 94** Texas Highways Magazine; **p. 96** Harvard Community Health Plan; **p. 99** Center For Disease Control; **p. 100** © Peter Vandermark/Stock, Boston

Notes

Notes